the houseboat book

by BARBARA FLANAGAN

photographs by ANDREW GARN

UNIVERSE

the houseboat book

by Barbara Flanagan

photographs by Andrew Garn

DEDICATION

*This book is dedicated to my tall and amazing teenagers, Nat and Gillian,
as they go off to have great adventures far beyond this house.*

First Published in the United States of America in 2003 by
UNIVERSE PUBLISHING
A division of Rizzoli International Publications, Inc.
300 Park Avenue South, New York, NY 10010

2003 2004 2005 2006 2007 / 10 9 8 7 6 5 4 3 2 1

Hardcover ISBN 0-7893-0967-X
Paperback ISBN 0-7893-0989-0
LCCN 2003104738

Design by Duuplex

Printed in the United States

TITLE PAGE PHOTO
Houseboats at sunset, Florida Keys
TABLE OF CONTENTS PHOTO
Houseboats in China Basin, San Francisco

ACKNOWLEDGEMENTS

Without the spirited collaboration of so many houseboat residents all over North America, this book would have taken years to complete. Thank you for so much trust, spontaneity, eloquence, patience, herbal tea, homemade wine, and road directions.

In beautiful British Columbia, Canada, thank you Granville Island, Vancouver; Ladner, Langley, New Westminster, and Richmond. In the Pacific Northwest, many thanks to Seattle's Lake Union and Portage Bay, and to all the houseboaters in Portland, as well as those on Oregon's Columbia, Willamette, and John Day rivers and sloughs. Thanks to California's Bay Area, where the houseboats of Sausalito, unincorporated Marin County, Port San Pablo, San Francisco, and Redwood City have persisted. On the other side of the continent, where houseboats are rarer, thank you and good luck to the water residents of Miami and the Florida Keys, and to those in Brooklyn, on the Hudson River, and near Atlantic City, New Jersey.

To all the North American houseboat communities not included in this book—in Toronto, along the Northeastern coast, on Louisiana bayous, in Southern California, along the Mississippi, and throughout the deltas of the Sacramento and other rivers—please email photographs to bflanagan@rcn.com and another book may appear someday. You never know.

Houseboat historian and longtime water resident Phil Frank, of Sausalito, was very generous in providing historical documents, photographs, and explanations. I am also grateful to the Sausalito Historical Society. Thanks, too, to Jan McFarland in Seattle. Pieter Sijpkes, the McGill architecture professor who thinks Montreal's Lachine Canal would be a perfect home for houseboats, allowed me to use his own photos taken for his houseboat studio. Attika Architekten, the Amsterdam architecture firm, readily shared information about their work and that of other water enthusiasts. Planning and building officials in several cities helped clarify many issues.

Thanks to Dan Wittenberg and his staff, to John and Trish Best at Sea Village, to T.J. Nelson, to Will and Barb Watkins, and to Rick Miner. I am also indebted to urbanist Jeff Fleeman of Berkeley. Kathryn Masi, architecture graduate student, completed invaluable research during her F.A. internship. Grazie!

I would like to thank the Canada Tourism Commission; Air Canada; Kate Colley Lo of Tourism Vancouver; the Portland Oregon Visitors Association; Joan Hallinan at Hallock Modey, Portland; and Maggie Pearson at Stuart Newman Associates, Miami.

For their gracious welcomes, I would like to thank The Avalon Hotel and Spa, Portland; Watertown, Seattle; the Ace Hotel, Seattle; Cypress House, Key West; and the Westin Grand, Vancouver.

Barbara Lowenstein is a wonderful literary agent and all-around sage. Very tall thanks to John Rogers. Thanks, Norman Kurz. And thank you, in advance, Jere Couture. And Richard too.

Many thanks to Stephen Schmidt (cool design); to Octavio Gonzalez (elements of style); and to Pam Somers (action). For ace photo researching, thank you Malado Baldwin and Dawn Bossman.

I am grateful to Rizzoli publisher Charles Miers, and to my editor Stephen Case, who welcomed the book from the get-go, and guided it with grace and intelligence. Thanks to Andrew Garn for getting to like houseboats, and for taking wonderful photographs—from many precarious boats and perches—without losing balance or focus.

And for overall sagesse, thank you Steve Zipperstein—again. For their fast and honest editorial acumen, and 24/7 consulting on all subjects, thanks to pros Irene Bender and Diane Zipperstein. And, to the AI staff, Nat and Gillian Weiner, let's do another book right now!

Barbara Flanagan

table of contents

Everything looks different from the water.
A Sausalito houseboat neighborhood seen
from a kayak.

preface

Fresh from architecture school, and working in the tony design department of Skidmore Owings and Merrill, San Francisco, I could barely afford bus fare downtown from my rented, Haight-Ashbury Victorian, let alone architecture of my own innovation (or renovation, for that matter.) Creative angst—a desire to own, plus the will to rehab—led me to check out a "houseboat" ad from the classifieds.

The "neighborhood" was perfect: a tiny marina on Mission Creek; a channel slicing through China Basin; an elegant, monotone landscape of maritime cranes, bridges, and warehouses. The dark but harmless gray underside of America's cutest, multi-colored city had a wonderfully secret, off-limits feel. From the boat I could see the skyline of pre-cast concrete high-rises we were erecting. (It looked better at night.)

It was the late 1970s, and so was the houseboat—a small, heavily shingled mansard roof-on-a-raft. The thing dipped when I stepped aboard. Although the place looked neither appetizing nor legal, I wanted to make it my own. The price (was it $15,000 or $50,000?) seemed high for a dump, but negligible compared to city real estate. What a find. Based in that downtown-adjacent unit, I'd be a corporate drafter by day and a bohemian artist by night.

It didn't take much due diligence to discover that a houseboat was not real estate. There could be no mortgage, no home insurance, and no tax savings, since the thing was taxed as a boat. Furthermore, there was no guarantee that the boat would float much longer. Prudent and chicken-hearted, I demurred.

Later, I went on to buy bankable real estate and raise a family with devoted normality in a monumental, brick Victorian house, in an historic neighborhood, in an affordable state. But I was haunted by two voices. One said, "Stay safe, dry, and consider resale"; the other said, "Live large, get wet."

The voice also said, "Buy an extremely cool, fiberglass kayak (21 inches by 18 feet) and learn how to paddle long distances down urban rivers and bays—the Hudson, East, Harlem, Delaware, and Lehigh Rivers, and Long Island Sound." (Circumnavigating Manhattan took one day, and thirty miles.)

The water was great, but the land was startling. Vast banks of industrial land reverted to wilderness. Basins and ports, cut and dredged for huge ships, looked like ruins of Roman concrete. And while the shorelines became quieter, the water was being churned by a new kind of recreation—speedboats and personal watercraft (Jet Skis)—using greater speed and noise than anything on the water before, including the tankers. If the water needed stewards, and it seems that it did, why not re-colonize the rough stretches with floating communities naturally interested in protecting the water environment?

Houseboats led me back to China Basin where I reunited with my un-bought mansard, or its identical twin, on its way to oblivion, and met the man replacing it.

The irony was rich. It had taken almost twenty-five years for houseboats to approach the respectability of landed houses—able to plug into utilities, pay taxes, and get insured. But the higher status, and much higher demand, came at a time when houseboat communities all over the world were imperiled by government bans, or rising prices. Amazingly, the twenty-plus mismatching houseboats on Mission Creek have been spared (for the sake of cultural diversity), while the industrial district was completely leveled to make way for Mission Bay—a 300-acre development of 6,100 housing units and six million square feet of office and retail space. The marina's new neighborhood will be a 43-acre biotech campus of the University of California.

A young computer entrepreneur bought my homely houseboat for well over $200,000. He plans to junk it to make way for his new dwelling—having just purchased a custom concrete barge for $20,000–30,000—and plans to rally friends to help him build a new house on top.

Among his neighbors is Jeremy Saxon, a musician/messenger who has floated on Mission Creek for twenty years. He explained the challenge to come. "To live on a houseboat, you not only have to change your life," Saxon says. "You have to change your idea of what life is about."

OPPOSITE *Everything looks different from a houseboat. Seattle's preserved Gasworks, a park with rusty ruins, seen from a Lake Union houseboat.*

introduction

Pursue something you love, and the rewards of the search will be better than you could imagine.

That is the message repeated by hundreds of people all over North America, who told me why floating on water was such a wonderful way to live, and why houseboat neighborhoods were the tightest and most neighborly communities they had ever joined, and why it took such a leap of faith to get there.

In the beginning, the path to these houseboats was tortuous. They were invisible: hidden behind dikes and sea walls; below bridges and highways; alongside railyards and industrial districts. Others are rural outposts—in places once reserved for hardcore fishing and logging, or heavy industry. They were unmapped and unlisted. The research was detective work, pieced together by clues and word-of-mouth. Know any houseboats in town? Down the river? Who owns the water? That some of the answers (rumored or in print) were inconsistent or contradictory made sleuthing a challenge. But usually, every time a person or reference contributed a fact, new territory opened up. Someone in New York saying "I heard of one marina in Portland" turned into, "Sure, we've got 3,000 houseboats here in Portland, but nobody seems to know!"

I questioned tow boat captains, fishermen, real estate agents, tourism officials, city planners, waiters, marina owners, architects, every friend near a body of water—and of course, houseboat residents themselves—on how to find more houseboats, and write their unwritten histories.
In return, everyone unfamiliar with houseboats asked why I was chasing a subject of such abject funkiness. Houseboaters, meanwhile, opened their houses on the spur of the moment to hours of invasion—shooting, talking, posing, tour-guiding. Some said they felt privileged to live where they lived, that they were grateful for the chance to explain what living on water is really like, and why the simplicity it engenders is so magnificent.

OPPOSITE *Beyond Vancouver, a wonderfully eclectic village of houseboats—sequestered but friendly— floats just beyond a Fraser River bank where the landscape is all mountains and forest.* **LEFT** *The real character of houseboats, and their residents, is revealed on the water side. This exuberant place faces downtown from Lake Union, Seattle.*

The people who talked about this simplicity were very different—millionaire college drop-outs, ascetic Ph.D.s, artists and bankers, kids and 88-year-olds—but they all repeated the same words.

The place made them *happy*, they said. Some had already lived the fully-loaded American dream before downsizing; some had never been tempted. But none of them had ever found a *sense of community* as convincing, nor could they explain how such independent and dissimilar types could live in such closely packed neighborhoods—*villages*, really—within small quarters, and feel so compelled to fend for one another. They also said they feel like *part of nature*, as seasonal shifts of wildlife check in and out, and weather holds them in its thrall.

Happiness? There was a question we never posed in architecture school: How do you make people happy? How do you make houses that help people care about unlikely neighbors, and the local animals, too? How do you design a community that says "we're all in this together"—this dock, this river, this city, and these land masses in between the oceans, too.

Now that I've visited so many happy villages, where the sense of community combines with being part of nature, I feel like Archimedes, accidentally discovering the key to buoyancy while bathing, then jumping out of the tub, and dashing around town shouting, "Eureka!"

While not looking for one, I found a tenet: Figure out what you love, then don't let it scare you away from living with it, among it, or on it. Carpe Diem.

what is a houseboat?

"Do people really live there?"

There is the mysterious black *peniche* parked like a waiting limousine along a Parisian *quai*, or the brightly painted roof garden blooming on an Amsterdam canal, or the floating village of junks in Hong Kong harbor, or the "Sleepless Dock" seen from a Seattle tour boat.

Houseboats are the story vehicles of two cinematic thrillers and two romantic comedies. In *Houseboat* and *Sleepless in Seattle*, Cary Grant and Tom Hanks each plays a responsible but over-wrought man who demonstrates his latent adventurousness to a spirited woman (Sophia Loren and Meg Ryan, respectively) by owning a floating cottage. In both films, the houseboat is like a deserted island—lovely, but incomplete without a pair of lovers abandoning themselves to mutual discovery and the vagaries of nature.

In *Cape Fear*, the original film noir and its remake, the role of the houseboat (a bona fide, boat-like houseboat this time) is more sinister. A family moves from their sprawling estate to their little vacation houseboat in order to lure and entrap a stalker. In a chilling turn of events, however, the stalker imprisons the family in the boat while a stormy river hurtles it downstream—and, in the remake, finally tears it apart.

In the same way that houseboats have represented romance and danger, good and bad, in film history, they have inspired strong emotions, love or hate, during the past two hundred years of our shared history.

OPPOSITE *Off Key West, this thatched, shack-style cabin—floating alone on a shallow reef—is an island's island.* **RIGHT** *This* factory-made houseboat *shares a Key West marina with stick-built dwellings called* houseboats or floating homes.

Houseboats have also been catalysts for passionate political drama in the public realm: expensive lawsuits, civil disobedience, and neighborhood strife—such as the hippie-era "Houseboat Wars" in Sausalito—over zoning, aesthetics, water rights, and environmental issues, old and new. Houseboat residents love their houseboats, but nearby landowners and bureaucrats have been known to dislike them for the evasion they flaunt.

For most North Americans, houseboats have remained a sort of fictional, or fantasy, form of housing—experienced vicariously via DVDs, travel channels, and vacation trips—but almost universally underestimated and misunderstood as a way of life.

According to houseboat veterans, the elusive appeal of the lifestyle lies not in the houseboat itself, but in the ever-changing territory outside it: the dense neighborhood of docks and boats set against vast expanses of blue firmament merging with wavy blue water. The smaller the houseboat, the more dramatic the experience may be. It represents a perch on a plane much grander, and more intricate, than any landed unit can deliver.

But what, precisely, is a *houseboat*? Definitions vary according to the age and address of the houseboat resident answering the question. The oldest hold-outs of the Sausalito marinas remember the bohemian years—1950s-1970s—when water-squatting artists and adventurers sal-

vaged parts, transforming army surplus boats into homemade, habitable art, now called houseboats, currently being replaced by expensive *floating homes*. In Sausalito, *houseboat* remains a term of endearment—a tribute to the legendary hipness of that town. The term is freely used by all, including recent *arrivistes*, to describe their costly, but landless, real estate.

At Canoe Pass, the river-top subdivision near Vancouver, residents own *float homes* alighting on water leased from the Canadian federal government. Call those units *houseboats* and the homeowners will launch into defensive tutorials. Theirs is among the most master-planned floating communities on the continent. Fully insured, conventionally mortgaged, and fully connected to amenities and municipal services, the float homes—built on buoyant, "permanent" concrete foundations—were designed as the antithesis to free-floating houseboats and their unstable heritage.

During the 1930s, a strange North American houseboat hybrid emerged: a modernized cabin structure attached to pontoons. The designs were refined and engineered; the first factory-made, steel-hulled houseboats appeared in the 1950s. Since then, dozens of factories have been manufacturing molded fiberglass and aluminum models.

The contemporary cruising houseboat is a wide and slow-moving power boat propelled by an inboard or outboard engine, with a relatively flat hull and shallow draft designed for short-term living and light cruising on inland lakes, rivers, canals, and bays. It is built for comfort, not for speed, on protected waters—a distinction that distances it from ocean-going cruisers and sailboats. Compared to *real* boats, houseboats are capacious, domestic, and easy to operate—hardly the preferred neighbors of skilled sailors and sportsmen. Nevertheless, because houseboats are registered as vessels, they find berth space more easily than non-powered floating dwellings, which are banned in some states and restricted in others.

On the following pages, the term *houseboat* will be used loosely and generically—with apologies to defenders of float homes—to describe any home that floats on purpose. In order to present some of the least-documented of floating dwellings, the following pages will be devoted mainly to floating homes. But before we narrow the subject, and at the risk of increasing confusion, here is a brief history of houseboat taxonomy.

In the lingo of marinas the understanding is simple. Houseboats propel themselves. Floating homes have no motor; they are moveable, but need to be towed over long distances, or manually maneuvered over short ones.

The difference is also visible. Houseboats usually look like boats, and floating homes look like houses. But this is a relatively new phenomenon. During the turn of the century, wealthy families escaped from city heat on navigable houseboats, or *arks*, designed as frilly vacation cottages. Floating houses, on the other hand, sometimes masqueraded as ships for the sake of style. Each was custom-built.

ABOVE *In Canoe Pass, Ladner, B.C., a three-level pavilion overlooks the Fraser River with wrap-around balconies.* **OPPOSITE TOP** *In San Francisco's Mission Creek marina, the houseboat dock is dotted with converted boats, increasingly historic, saved from oblivion by water dwellers.* **OPPOSITE LEFT** *Houseboat as roof: a do-it-yourself experiment in Key West.*

The popularity of houseboating as a transient vacation adventure burgeoned during the 1960s and 70s and claimed "houseboat" as a term for factory-made vessels. Soon, real estate brokers and homeowners' associations began using the term "floating home" to describe house-like water dwellings that were gaining in popularity and value as moorage spaces became rare.

Most floating homes are conventionally built, wood-frame houses attached to a means of flotation—called a barge, raft, platform, hull, or simply "flotation," depending on the people who make it and the materials they use: logs, concrete, Styrofoam, plastic barrels, steel, or fiberglass—all in different shapes and combinations. Connections separate houseboats from floating homes. Houseboats, like other boats, are designed to be self-sufficient when underway via power generators, water storage tanks, and marine toilets with holding tanks that can be emptied at pump-out stations. When they moor, houseboats also have the option of hooking up to marina services—electrical, water, sewage, cable, or satellite. Floating homes in residential marinas, on the other hand, are "permanently" connected to services via conduits and PVC pipes, rigid or flexible, running under the docks. (The house can be easily disconnected if it changes slips.)

Sewage treatment differs with location. Some marinas can pump waste directly into the city sewer; others pump it from the houses to their own interim treatment station before pumping it into the sewer—or in rural areas, into their own facilities. A few unimproved marinas may offer limited services while being brought up to local codes. In Sausalito, one small co-op marina has no hook-ups, just water hoses and extension cords on the dock, and a waste holding tank on land.

Just as the distinctions between motorized houseboats and non-motorized floating homes can be confusing, the differences between modern, code-compliant floating dwellings and code-flaunting floating units are even hazier. Just because a house looks like house does not mean it obeys community rules of health and safety. This is not a good time for confusion. In the housing industry, standardization and homogeneity reign. Insurance companies, financial institutions, and government agencies want to know how to categorize all types of housing "product" in order to process their paperwork more easily: policies, loans, permits, and taxes. While houseboats may no longer break codes of sanitation and construction, they are non-compliant with the tenor of the times: conformity and uniformity.

Houseboaters comprise a dispersed, if enthusiastic, community competing for limited marina space with bigger interests: fishing, tourism, leisure boating, port authorities, and real estate. No matter that water neighborhoods have earned their keep, and raised their status, by attracting wealthy taxpayers, paying tourists, and productive citizens. Houseboats have become an endangered species.

With the hope that familiarity will encourage more houseboat communities, here is a brief field guide to the surviving water dwellings of North America.

BOAT DWELLINGS

These structures began as boats, but have been recruited, or redesigned, to serve as dwellings. Some move, others cannot. All have hulls.

LIVE-ABOARD

A live-aboard may be a sailor taking a break between continents, or a retiree living full-time. In marinas, they are allowed, banned, or tolerated (with a *don't ask, don't tell* policy). Although this little-known, international population comprises a potential citizenry for floating homes, live-aboards are not well-documented here because they are officially boats.

BOAT CONVERTED TO HOME

This is a live-aboard that can no longer cruise, move, or keep on pretending it is a boat, when it's really a dwelling. It may look like an active boat from the outside, but on the inside it has been modified for permanent residence.

FUSION

Part boat, part house, this is a boat substantially transformed by retro-fits and appendages, and much too domestic to be mistaken for a functional boat.

FACTORY-MADE HOUSEBOATS

A factory-made hybrid (a livable boat), introduced in the 1950s, designed for vacation living and light cruising on calm waters. Vintage houseboats are charming, overlooked examples of this design, endearing as Airstream trailers.

LEFT *A boat domesticated by appendages—or fusion—on False Creek, Vancouver.* **OPPOSITE TOP** *A boat converted to home commands the view of Vancouver's costly view condos.* **OPPOSITE BOTTOM** *A factory-made houseboat in Key West, and a funky fusion of salvaged hull and house parts in Sausalito.*

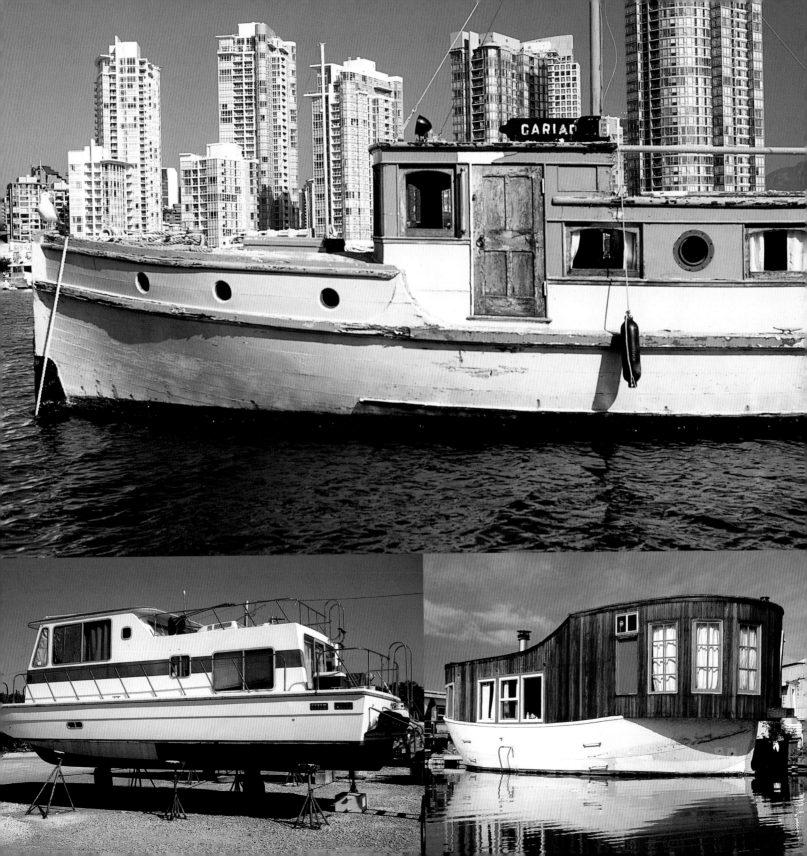

FLOATING HOMES

These are non-motorized dwellings—built on flotation bases—designed to remain in slips where they will be connected to water, electrical, and sewage services. They are best categorized not by architectural styles, but by individual form and function.

CABIN

A small, rustic shelter with a deliberately primitive look, built using the simplest materials (usually wood) and construction methods.

COTTAGE

A more neighborly version of a cabin, small, but intricately detailed. Painted or planted to look charming and neighborly.

SUBURBAN HOUSE

A floating house designed as a respectable version of a middle-class suburban home. It conveys the message: We are not misfits.

TOWNHOUSE

Marinas are like townhouse neighborhoods: Narrow parcels (slips) flanked by houses on both sides. Some floating homes conform to this form of urban living with two-story townhouselike floor plans, solid side walls, open front and rear elevations, and flat roofs.

PAVILION

Like a free-standing temple, this house takes advantage of the multidimensional views from water locations.

EXOTICA

A house that illustrates its owners' travels or interests in other places with architectural references, though not necessarily by exact reproduction. Thai, Tibetan, Indian, Chinese, and Japanese are some of the more popular influences.

SHOWPLACE

Function be damned. This is a dreamhouse, palace, or extravagant folly that may have everything (or nothing) to do with water living. It is a spectacular landmark.

BOX

Minimal shelter, minimal design, often made with salvaged material. Built expeditiously and interesting for its guilelessness. The opposite of a showplace.

SCULPTURE

The opposite of the box. It is all-design design: a striking, artistic form that also happens to be a house.

ASSEMBLAGE

An accumulation of materials, artifacts, collections, and plants that obscure the structure of the house underneath. Like a work of art—intentionally or by accident.

VEHICLE

A van, trailer, train car, or mobile home attached to a floating base. Often enlarged, or simply inhabited.

EXPERIMENT

The house is shaped by a series of functional trials, artistic experiments, or both. Usually a work in progress.

history

Are houseboats older than civilization? Proof is scarce, but the attraction of water living must have been strong back when waterways were the only place one could flee enemies, fetch water, fish, and seek out new trading posts and hunting grounds—simultaneously. Water also obviated the need for turf (or cave) disputes.

The earliest buoyant architecture biodegraded much faster than the marble variety, so its heritage exists mainly in story (Noah's Ark) and naval art (Egyptian). But all over the world, traditional water communities, unchanged for centuries, suggest that humans have always had compelling reasons to float.

The Marsh Arabs (*Madan*) of southern Iraq, formerly Lower Mesopotamia, have been building all-grass floating architecture and infrastructure for at least as long as the Sumerians documented them—over 5,000 years ago. The Madan tied reeds together to form thick columns, and used them as structural ribs to form grand, arched spaces. The dwellings, made of the same material, rested on floating islands, serving as farmyards and moorage for their working boats. Until recent political turmoil began to destroy their habitat, the Madan were self-sufficient, and self-sustaining, in ways that render their *primitive* floating life sophisticated by progressive standards.

In 1916 Gertrude Bell wrote this journal passage:

> We went up the Euphrates all morning. It is the most curious sight. The whole country is under water, the villages, which are mainly not sedentary but nomadic, are built on floating piles of reed mats, anchored to palm trees, and locomotion is entirely by boat . . . The light and color are beyond belief—it's a landscape unlike any I have seen and of the strangest beauty . . . reed architecture has many possibilities and can be quite imposing.

It is also unbelievable that so many millennia of elegant shelter remained unknown to the West before it reached near-extinction. Somehow the study of floating architecture seems to have slipped the attention of scholars. Too domestic to be honored as naval history, too indigenous to be treated as proper architecture, and often deemed too primitive to be promoted by governments trying to clear waterways for progress, houseboats have but three constituencies ready to defend them as part of our cultural heritage: other houseboaters, anthropologists, and foreign tourists who have helped their survival in many countries.

ASIA

Traditional houseboats with long histories occupy the waters of China, India, Thailand, Cambodia, and Vietnam. In some towns, houseboats are part of complex water communities where life is lived off-land. Water residents reach neighbors by walking boat-to-boat, or they maneuver their boats through water traffic to reach floating markets, where produce is sold and bought from boats. Vendor boats also deliver their wares to houseboats.

Vietnam has a wide range of houseboats, from "cottages" with thatched roofs lined up in street formation along the Mekong Delta, to brightly painted houseboats with high wooden hulls, to colorful box-shaped houses on floating platforms moored among the tall islands of Halong Bay, to the smallest boats, with arching roofs, seen throughout Southeast Asia.

Among the earliest documented water dwellings are family work boats. The vessels held minimal living quarters to reserve maximum space for the owner's livelihood: fishing, trading, or transporting cargo. The idea of using a home as the means of earning a living, and vice versa, is an ancient idea that seems to have originated in China. Along the Yangtze River, and in Hong Kong's Aberdeen Harbor, traditional fishing boats (junks) raft up together to form "floating cities." In 1901, a Western writer wrote about a place where "four hundred thousand live . . . daily rising and falling with the tide" outside Canton: "These boats are homes in which millions of human beings have been born, have lived and have died . . . in many cases without ever having set foot on land."[1]

Cargo houseboats have also had a long history in Thailand and India. In Thailand, small tugboats pull caravans of large, wood-hulled cargo houseboats—with arched corrugated steel roofs—along the Chao Phraya River. In Bangkok, the city canals (klongs) still hold houseboats functioning as small food markets. In Kashmir (the state of Jammu and Kashmir), cargo houseboats shaped like long, shingled cabins on upswept barges and called *bahats* have transported building materials along the Jelhum River. *Dungas*, smaller versions of *bahats*, have been used for living but not hauling.

The most famous and profitable houseboats of Kashmir are in the city of Srinagar, where tourism has been an important industry: Growing over the last century, but

OPPOSITE TOP *Houseboats in India. Left: Retired cargo houseboats called* kettuvalloms *now take tourists on river trips through Kerala; the boats look like arched baskets. Right: Cargo houseboats—bahats and dungas—ply the canals of Srinagar, Kashmir.*
OPPOSITE BOTTOM *In Srinagar, "hotel houseboats," rented by tourists, are known for their carved woodwork and ornate textiles inside and out.*

declining in recent years. There, hundreds of houseboats, or "floating palaces," are permanently moored throughout the mazelike waters of Dal Lake and Nagin Lake, waiting for international travelers. The elaborate barge-mansions—15 to 20 feet wide and 60 to 150 feet long—are made of teaklike Indian hardwood, carved in intricate patterns, and furnished in Indian/Victorian décor. Tourists are delivered to the houseboats via *shikara* (gondola-like boats), and the small boats return to sell merchandise, or offer tours of the floating markets and floating gardens.

In a twist of fate, the Srinagar houseboats, created by a political dispute, are now endangered by one. In the late 1880s, the British wanted to build houses in the cool climate, but the local Maharaja denied them land ownership. In response, the colonists built on the water. Today, the conflict between India and Pakistan is resulting in a decline in the tourist revenue that once preserved and expanded the houseboat architecture.

In Kerala, another part of India, another distinctive tradition of houseboats was revived by tourism. *Kettuvallams* were the cargo houseboats, made of anjili wood tied together with coir using a technique closer to basketry than carpentry. The large boats, up to eighty feet long, were difficult to construct, and heavy to move: they were poled by one or two strong men. When powerboats took over their loads of rice and coconuts, the old boats and their craftsmen began to disappear. The idea of rebuilding the boats for tourist cruises revived the craft, and created employment in the backwaters.

Varied as the Asian houseboats may be—in form, size, craftsmanship, and social rank—they share at least one intriguing trait. They look very lived-in. All of them respond to heat, humidity, and location in different ways, with materials (and a daily adaptability) unfamiliar to Westerners. When identical vessels raft up, you see how each owner has altered his vessel to make shade and vent breezes. Asian houseboats use textiles like building materials; building materials like textiles; and both textiles and building materials like clothing—layering, draping, sun-shading, decorating, and marking seasonal changes. Many of the houseboats are topped with a skeletal framework designed to hold these temporary materials. Woven grass matting, hung from poles, become roofs and awnings on some Kashmiri work boats. (On traditional *dunga* houseboats, removable plank siding helps ventilate air.) Houseboat hotels are a completely different, ostentatious category. In the high summer season, they are dressed in a remarkable collection of useful, festive textiles: scalloped roof and veranda canopies, awnings, umbrellas, and outdoor draperies.

Chinese junks, rafted up, form a chaotic patchwork of textiles and new tarps that have replaced grass matting and palm leaves. In Thailand, the materials are even more unruly. Ramshackle as they may appear, their simple, arched structures create flexibility at low cost. Ribs of metal or wood form a fixed framework to hold layers of moveable, flexible materials. The panels drape over the arches to form both roofing and siding. Panels of metal (lightweight corrugated steel) and panels of fabric are used in the same way. They can roll up, or slide aside to create an open boat (like a convertible car, top down); or the steel can be curled up (like the top of a sardine can) to create a door or window. In this way the houseboat can react to sun and winds, and the circumstances of different mooring positions.

OPPOSITE TOP *Most* peniches (French cargo houseboats) *moored along the Seine's stone* quais *are now full-time dwellings.* **OPPOSITE BOTTOM** *"Little Venice" on Regent's Canal in London.*

EUROPE

Europe has a long history of houseboats working its network of canals and rivers. Best known are the cargo-hauling *peniches* in France, *narrow boats* in Britain, and *tjalk* in the Netherlands. Belgium and Sweden share similar histories of barges working their canals.

Very different than the Asian boats, European "canal boats" resemble floating rooftops revealing little domestic commotion, especially in winter. Today many of those vessels have also changed jobs; they have been renovated as small floating inns, or as houseboats designed for cruising by foreign tourists on vacation. Those converted to single-family dwellings—with living quarters and cargo hold combined into a large space—are very long, skinny versions of industrial lofts, surprisingly spacious.

In Amsterdam and Paris, houseboats have been a familiar part of the tourist scenery for decades. After World War II, when housing was scarce and retired *tjalk* were plentiful, Amsterdam officials encouraged the renovation of barges and allowed them to moor along the canals. The barges share the water with two other types of floating houses: A "house vessel" is a hybrid—basically a dwelling using an old boat hull as flotation. An "ark" is a long, shoebox-shaped house sitting on a rectangular floating foundation, concrete or steel, shaped to fit. In Amsterdam's greater metropolitan area, there are over 2,000 floating dwellings.

Paris is a paradise for *peniches* since they moor along the wide, romantic *quais,* far below the noisy street level. Many of the old barges were scrapped, and many of the remaining non-working *peniches*—and the limited mooring space—have soared in value over the last thirty years. The Port of Paris estimates that there are about 1,000 dwellings on the three city rivers.

Birmingham, England, once the fire pit of the industrial revolution, now sees itself as a brick-walled Venice, laced with canals—the old roadways of commerce. Today, houseboats have plenty of mooring space along the docks, illustrating how charming the old factory city has become.

For years, the canals and harbors of Copenhagen have welcomed a small number of working houseboats and boat dwellings, as well as architect-designed floating houses. Now the city and port are collaborating on a plan to enliven abandoned wharfs by building new floating dwellings for households of different sizes and incomes.

For centuries, reclaiming land from the sea has been a national mission in the Netherlands. The Dutch have routed water, and reshaped dirt into an impeccably engineered and constantly maintained landscape of canals and building parcels—one wet, the other dry. Lately, however, the Dutch have reversed their thinking and are building right on the water they had been fighting. The government is exploring, and actually mandating, creative construction—floating on water or held on pilings—in striking architectural forms. In 2001, a complete neighborhood of "water houses" being built in Ijburg, a new district of Amsterdam, started with the opening of six floating houses, designed as prototypes and temporary sales center. Although the Dutch are experts in boat-living, they have consulted with North Americans as the authorities on floating houses. What the Dutch, in turn, contribute is an irrepressible sense of experimentation: housing designed for its time with new materials, vibrant colors, flexible floor plans, pre-fab structure, pre-fab baths, and configurations that make creative use of the water and docks.

OPPOSITE *In Amsterdam, the demand for houseboat living far exceeds supply although a couple thousand vessels line many miles of canals in the old city and beyond. This canal is the scenic Prinsengracht.*

OPPOSITE *Larkspur, 1910. Late in the 19th century, wealthy San Franciscans created a seasonal summer colony of "arks"—floating cabins anchored in the bay.* **ABOVE** *Vancouver, 1895. Lumbermen of British Columbia and the Pacific Northwest floated cabins on cedar logs to make fast, moveable work camps in the mid-1800s.*

NORTH AMERICA

The canal era of the United States is not a glorious one. Only two decades after an expensive water network was finally excavated, the arrival of railroads rendered mule-pulled barges obsolete by the mid-nineteenth century. Nevertheless, "canal boats" or "barges" were family-operated cargo houseboats designed for the same purpose as their precursors in China, Thailand, and India—keeping the family together in a traveling trade. Now that canals and docks are gradually being re-filled and restored as "heritage corridors" in the U.S. and Canada, they are ready to welcome an emerging kind of North American tourism: exploring the countryside by newly manufactured motorized houseboats.

While North America was expanding its transportation system during the mid-1800s, it was also felling trees to build new towns. In British Columbia, Canada, and the Pacific Northwest in the U.S., timber companies built floating logging camps to move loggers along the shorelines, where they could cut trees and move them directly into the water, where they would then be tied into log rafts and towed to lumber mills. The camps started out as all-male work dorms for loggers, but later grew into villages, complete with wives and children. Floating houses were joined by floating cookhouses, hotels, and general stores, all reached by boat. At night, the water location probably discouraged resident grizzly bears from chasing the marauders off their land. Some camps survived well into the mid-twentieth century.

Throughout North America's ports, people working on boats have often lived in their workplaces, or on smaller boats nearby, for economy and convenience. They have also modified boats—seaworthy and not—into permanent homes. The proliferation of floating houses in Vancouver, Seattle, and Portland—starting in the late nineteenth century and flourishing until the mid-twenti-eth century—may be explained by the laws of supply and demand: the supply of cedar logs usable for floating foundations, and the demand from large numbers of maritime workers—boat-builders, fishermen, millworkers—to live near their jobs. Photographs of Seattle's Lake Union, taken in the early 1900s, show the lakefront crowded with fishing boats, each with its own floating cabin acting as home and moorage. Although many of the boats were gone by the 1930s, the Depression created a new demand for basic shelter. Houseboats in Seattle, and throughout the west, became a way to escape rent and taxes, and the seamy underground reputation persisted until much later.

In Portland, Oregon, the history of floating architecture from industrial sheds to luxurious homes forms an evolutionary panorama along the waterfronts of the Columbia and Willamette rivers.

Sausalito, California's precious bayside village at the sunny end of San Francisco's Golden Gate Bridge, tried and failed to be become the Pittsburgh of the West in the late nineteenth century. A three-year boom finally arrived

OPPOSITE TOP *Winter houseboating on the Miami River was once an exotic Florida tradition.* **OPPOSITE BOTTOM** *In the 1880s, San Franciscans towed summer arks into the Bay and left this landscape untouched. Today, things are reversed: the Bay is wide open and the hills are bristling with houses. This view is from Tiburon, 1895.*

with World War II when 75,000 people arrived in the county to work at Marinship, the 200-acre Bechtel plant erected to build Liberty ships. The government built thousands of pre-fab housing units on what is now Marin City. After the war, a housing shortage required some resourcefulness, and former ship workers built dwellings from surplus military boats and parts. Much of that historical debris is still visible, continuously being restored and preserved in the oldest and most venerable houseboats of Marin County.

The Bay Area was already famous for an inventive form of floating community long before the ship surplus arrived. Unlike most water dwellings, these had nothing to do with work or hardship. They were pleasure houseboats supporting a summertime water culture of leisure and sport.

In the 1880s, hunters started building vessels—part duck blind, part hunt club—to be towed into the Bay. These rectangular wooden "arks" were designed with flat bottoms like the local cargo boats, but were meant for play. The voyages became more elaborate as wealthy San Franciscans gradually formed a floating summer colony of arks near Belvedere, across the Bay from Sausalito. From the 1890s to the early 1900s, about forty arks of different sizes and intentions (family arks and bachelor arks) would array themselves in cliques and stay put all season, using rowboats to visit one another. Husbands commuted to the city via steam launch each day, while wives masterminded social lives. Each morning, tradesmen took grocery orders

by boat and delivered in time for dinner. Boatmen also delivered water and picked up trash.

The typical ark had a slightly arched roof extending over open decks on all sides. Shipwrights built most of the arks like the interiors of Victorian ships with tongue-and-groove interior surfaces and space-saving elements: built-in furniture and storage, and windows that vanished into the walls. The ark dwellers designed their own spectacles including plein-air concerts on floating barges, punctuated by fireworks, and surrounded by arks flying family flags and illuminated by Chinese lanterns for the occasion.

Florida was home to early pleasure-seeking houseboaters. In the first decade of the twentieth century, wealthy Northerners found the protected waters of Miami's Biscayne Bay perfect for entertaining friends in large houseboats during the winter. In the shallow water, private clubs were built on "stilts," and the houseboats could "island hop" without leaving the Bay. Today, the remaining structures of "Stiltsville" lie empty, ready for rehabilitation and cultural interpretation by the federal government, which owns the property.

Certainly, the preservation of houseboats as testaments to the ingenuity, architectural diversity, and indefatigable optimism of Asians, Europeans, and North Americans, cannot be far behind.

1. James Ricalton. *China Through the Stereoscope: A Journey Through the Dragon Empire at the time of the Boxer Uprising.* New York: Underwood & Underwood, 1901.

Amplified by the glow of sky on water, all sunsets are worth watching. **OPPOSITE** *In Key West, pastel houseboat reflections sweeten the spectacle.* **RIGHT** *In the Pacific Northwest, natural woods cast golden colors.*

water

Why water? Houseboats always raise that question. Why would anyone leave the stability of terra firma to live on a moving surface, in smaller quarters, at greater expense and uncertainty?

The answer is simple. Water changes everything.

Water residents are water lovers, and water lovers adore water with a passion incomprehensible to all but those who share their passion. Like any love, it can only be described by rhapsodizing, using a language thick with clichés. (If you know it words are inadequate; if you don't know it words are irrelevant.) To avoid all that, water lovers joke about their condition, seeing it as both a powerful curse and blessing, calling themselves "water rats." To them, water is not an alien environment, but an alternative atmosphere, akin to liquid air, inhabited by intelligent creatures—dolphins, for instance—for whom they feel an eerie affinity.

Can someone who doesn't crave water understand the attraction? Houseboat owners, who have convinced friends or spouses to share floating spaces, say that time is key to understanding. The longer one lives on the water, the less one fears it, and the better one may adapt to watertop rhythms. But it's not for everyone: the most common way of saying that water obsessions are born, not made.

Movement is the issue. Houseboats and docks move. Other things traveling along the water—wind, boats, waterfowl—either make the houseboats move, or create that impression. Sometimes the movement is imperceptible. Sometimes one sees the movement (a swaying lamp), but doesn't feel it.

Larger houseboats may feel completely stable, but smaller ones bob in various ways, all of them delightful. If you love water, the motion is energizing; it puts the body on alert, electrifying all multi-sensory, neuromuscular systems, reminding us how sensitive our eyes, inner ears, knees, and feet really are. On land, it is easy to forget that feet are our sole physical connection to architecture. (Reflexologists, take note.)

Walking on docks also delivers an acoustical thrill. Like a drum, each section of dock—wood planks, plywood, solid metal, or grating—has a different sound, depending on the material, the size of the air chamber under it, or the mood of the water reflecting the sound upwards. Surfaces reverberate. So you hear your own footfalls within your whole body.

Weather intensifies the adventure. Storms churn the water, and turn up the percussion. Most houseboats "rock and roll"; all of them creak or groan as they strain against their moorings. Some residents admit that they relish the adventure of being walloped by nature (as long as their boat is ready for it). The drama has three acts: suspense, turmoil, survival. When high winds and waves strain the mooring lines, residents monitor each other's homes: a marina's greatest hazard is a boat that breaks loose and batters its neighbors. Every marina has its folk tales, real or exaggerated over time, of rescued boats and heroic neighbors—as well as the homes, sunk or flooded, that got away. Many houseboaters believe the ever-present threat of storms is the force that keeps houseboat marinas more cohesive than other communities.

Then again, it might be the air that hypnotizes residents to act differently than land-lubbers do. What is that fragrance: biomass, salted or unsalted? Some claim sea air is addictive because its molecules get ionized into a heady, invigorating cocktail that makes electrically stable land air taste stale by comparison. Even land lovers agree that sea air smells delicious.

Architecture is not the endpoint of the floating life. A dwelling is neither fortress nor estate, but more of a field station, outpost, or observation deck in an inexhaustibly fascinating terrain. The indoors exist only because of the outdoors. And since the location is all about personal obsession, residents tend to design and outfit their homes with an abandon seldom seen on land. Unfettered by property values (no land underneath them) or unknown neighbors, water residents express themselves with art, color, collections, and architectonic form. They also invent ceremonies and ways of socializing. They experiment. Houseboats are personal, opinionated compositions about living on water. In other words, a floating abode is not simply an homage to a certain lifestyle, it really *is* a lifestyle—bold living—in the fullest expression of the term.

The houseboat resident represents the opposite of the suburban McMansion household that buys an inflated unit on a denuded plot, generically subdivided. While McMansionites seek to buy distance—separation from the city, from lawn mates, and from lesser subdivisions— the houseboater looks for greater proximity to water. If getting close requires living within a few feet, or inches, from like-minded, water-obsessed people, so much the better. The ambience cancels out minor inconveniences.

In that respect, water living is like city living. The sense of co-habitation supersedes each individual. In addition, the unpredictable hazards of city living require street smarts

(water smarts?)—a heightened sense of physical awareness combined with everyday common sense. Somehow the combination of intensity and adversity create an esprit de corps that manages to bring together some very independent people with a tacit understanding: they will look after one another in the face of adversity, without invading mutual privacy.

Water acts as a great social leveler, a phenomenon that draws these remarkably eclectic citizens into communities of extreme architectural togetherness. This human variety, living within a density they casually endure, is an astounding sight in North America, where customers demand increasing size and uniformity in their cars, houses, stores, etc. Since houseboat living flouts all the marketing formulas telling consumers what type of *housing product* they want, it opens up major possibilities: What other kinds of eccentric dwellings might capture the public imagination? What if everyone born with an attachment to place—mountain, jungle, desert, city—lived in a home expressing their site-specific devotion? Or, more to the point, what happens if we run out of places to love, and are left only with housing product to live in!

Lovers of water fall into three categories. Full-immersion types like to get wet; surface types prefer to stay dry; others like both sides of the water. The full immersionists enjoy water sports—swimming, diving, surfing, snorkeling—and wear equipment that helps them look and act like the sea mammals they admire. Many admit that they would prefer to be in the water all the time.

Aquadynamic gear, such as fins, masks, wet suits, and breathing apparatus, helps them stay in the water longer, allowing themselves to feel lifted up, freed from gravity, and moved along by the rhythmic waves and currents. For immersion types, a state of full-body flotation is a magnificent experience.

Surface people prefer to use boats, rather than their bodies, to experience buoyancy. On top of the water, they enjoy a different kind of sensation, clear of everything but subtle and unpredictable movements. Laden with the raw smell of saltwater, wind almost becomes visible. Because the wind changes force and direction over the course of a day, as the earth warms and cools, other patterns shift, too: the sounds, smells, the very texture of the air. But water lovers also face two dilemmas: finding water and a way to get on it, and the storing and transporting of all their water gear. Houseboating puts everything where it ought to be—right *in* the water, inches away. Large bodies of water offer an incomparable experience for acrophilics. They are the only places on earth where the grandeur of endlessness becomes multi-dimensional.

Paddle a boat into a bay and you are dwarfed by tall skies reflected in an expanse of water. The sense of humility this engenders creates a wonderfully confusing thrill, intimidating but serene. When mountains are not visible, water is the best platform for viewing celestial panoramas. On a still day, sky and sea merge to form a continuous space of bright color (sky blue) or colorlessness (winter white), suspending you somewhere between earth and infinity, with miles of unknown depth just below.

Water lovers look at these great expanses with a unique perspective. Small things can seem portentous. Clouds mass; a pelican circles; a seal surfaces, disappears, then resurfaces far away. On water, the phenomena of daily life become ceremonial. A sunrise or sunset is routinely extraordinary, amplified by the glow of sky on water. Rain—the sound of water on water—becomes mesmerizing. In the Northeast, ice floes—a natural occurrence people on land seldom see—pass by their windows in the languid pace of parade floats.

Those big, bright expanses of uncluttered space give water residents a rare sort of relationship with light. In fact, light is one of the natural phenomena they describe with great enthusiasm. During the day, sunlight enters through skylights and windows, unobstructed by trees, hills, or tall buildings. Light also enters indirectly, reflected by the water surface, which in turn mirrors the sky. When the wind rakes the water, and the water reflects shifting clouds, the kinetic, tremulous patterns bounce onto the boats' interior walls (the swimming pool effect). Sunlight constantly shifts in color, with two or more sources of light changing throughout the day. While land houses have sun exposures, light, water houses work like projection screens for the moodiness of the weather, some of it barely perceptible, some extreme in its intensity.

Ordinary, artificial light becomes spectacular on the waterfront. At night, houses and docks become a pattern of glowing yellow dots and rectangles. Calm water reflects and expands the pattern; rippling water animates the pattern into a performance of dancing fountains or fireworks. As living on water persuades people to submit to its rhythms, they begin to enjoy the sensory, elusive joys of scenery without trying to own it or shape it. When water residents describe the extraordinary freedom of living on water, they talk about the relief of giving up land and all the maintenance it requires. Many never realized all the time spent irrigating and cultivating until they left their gardens behind, and with them the sounds of their neighbors: lawn mowers, leaf blowers, chainsaws. With the new freedom came free time.

On land, wildlife is usually the enemy. Deer, rabbits, and groundhogs eat gardens; gophers and geese ruin lawns. On water, an incredible array of wildlife—birds, mammals, fish, reptiles—makes fleeting appearances, most of them welcome.

Leaving cars behind is another liberation. In marinas, vibrations and traffic noises are distant, muffled by the wind, or by the sounds of water slapping against hulls. "Just walking away from my car onto the docks makes me feel like I've gone on vacation," says one floating home veteran. Other residents make the same observation, wishing they could understand the strange, magnetic influences at work: "Once I get here, out on the water, I don't want to leave."

Houseboaters say the absence of cars also lets residents grow closer. One cannot dart unseen directly from house to car, but must walk over the water separating the floating homes from the parking lots on land. The routes traversing the water—piers and docks—channel the residents into narrow common spaces where they meet or greet one another face to face, in broad daylight or in dim twilight.

ABOVE *The floating medium shapes houseboat life. Seattle's orderly houseboat neighborhoods are supported by calm, fresh, lake water.*
FOLLOWING PAGES *When San Francisco sunsets turn Mission Creek purple, the marina becomes a quaint village backlit by the big city.*

One of the most common misconceptions about water life is that it is all wet. Humid. Dank. What keeps water-top dwellings dry is the constant air movement, the enemy of mold. Only interiors sealed up for long periods of time become mildewy.

The form and character of a houseboat community is shaped by the kind of water surrounding it. Look careful-ly and you discover that watercourses have different flora, fauna, colors, speeds, temperatures, opacities, and cultur-al histories. They have different personalities. Some rivers are savagely beautiful; they rush along with a steady, insistent current, carrying silt and dangerous debris (logs, branches, etc.). Tidal rivers move up and down—quite dramatically—as well as downstream. Bays are more tem-pestuous; they are whipped up by storms, and boats are peeled or pitted by the corrosive action of seawater. Only freshwater lakes, where water stays in the same place, are benign.

The stability of the water may not fully explain why Seattle's floating home marinas, on peaceful Lake Union and its continuous Portage Bay, are among the oldest and best-organized floating villages in North America. But Seattle residents are particularly proud of their freshwater and the wildlife it attracts. There are neighborhood popu-lations of otter and beaver (evasive), and ducks and geese (invasive but welcome). Once people disappear, raccoons appear on the docks, swiping cat food if they can.

People swim quite fearlessly, using swim ladders on their decks, being careful not to disturb centuries' worth of industrial muck at the bottom. The water, brownish-

green and cold, is clear enough to see salmon swimming by. When residents tire of fishing, they catch "log lob-sters" (crawfish) in their sleep, by lowering a crawfish trap into the water before bed, and pulling it up in the morning. A local houseboaters' cookbook also recom-mends baiting them with salami on a string, or just snap-ping up any visible crawdads with kitchen tongs.

flotation

Flotation is the marvel of floating life. Buoyant dwellings prove one of the most magical and counter-intuitive rules of childhood science: Archimedes' principle guarantees that anything can float if it is shaped to displace its own weight in water.

The trick is to make the shape waterproof. Sound easy? Here are "Standards for Float Homes," an advisory guide from the Floating Home Association in Vancouver:

> The flotation devices shall be durable and not subject to deterioration by water, mechanical damage due to floating debris, electrolytic action, water-borne solvents, organic infestation, or physical abuse, to the satisfaction of a marine surveyor or professional engineer.

What the standards do not mention are the storms and accidental collisions everyone takes for granted. But therein lies the hidden challenge of floating architecture: engineering the submerged foundation.

This is one of the features separating factory-made houseboats from custom-made floating homes. Motorized, boatlike houseboats require maneuverable, lightweight hulls, or pontoons, designed to slice through protected waters using minimal fuel and to be towed along highways.

In North America, most floating homes mimic conventional wood-framed houses in style and construction. The difference lies just below the finished floor, or below the stringers, where the floating foundation begins. Above and below water, floating houses tend to be highly vernacular, using regional materials and methods. The base is usually a rectangular platform varying in depth from two to fifteen feet. It is often an ad-hoc assembly by the owner or local builders, in some ways more fascinating than the architecture it serves. (Scuba diving should be added to houseboat walking tours.) (Technically, a land-based house can be transformed into a floating home by having a house mover detach the wood-frame from its foundation, raise it on hydraulic jacks, truck it to the waterfront, lower it onto a barge, and launch it into the water.)

Crucial as it is to houseboat anatomy, the base has no common name. Each region shows a strong historical preference for one or two materials based on its maritime trades, chosen from a large variety of options: logs, lumber, steel, concrete, aluminum, fiberglass, Styrofoam, steel drums, or plastic barrels.

These materials form two kinds of bases: platform or hull. A platform carries liveable space on top of the water (à la Huck Finn's raft). A single hull usually encloses usable space beneath the surface of the water; multiple hulls (pontoons) may hold nothing but air. Concrete is a relatively new material for houseboat support, although concrete tankers and barges were built during the steel shortage of World War I. Portland cement, patented in

1824, is the ingredient giving "modern" concrete its important quality of not dissolving underwater. Hydration is the chemical reaction that turns the mixture of water and hydraulic cement into a dense mass. (Ancient Roman concrete used different ingredients.)

Other less durable materials need to be carefully maintained and monitored. Most need a protective coating to make them last. An older wooden hull needs hauling out for scraping and repainting every few years, or sooner. Saltwater reacts chemically with unprotected steel and aluminum, eroding hulls in short order. Styrofoam absorbs water and houses destructive algae if it is not sealed by concrete, fiberglass, or coal tar. In theory, even cedar logs, capable of lasting a century or more under fresh water, may attract termites and other wood-softening insects.

Certain flotation methods are being replaced with greener ones. In one Portland marina, the docks and some houses are supported by tubular rows of auto tires stacked like Lifesaver candies, injected or stuffed with foam. A landmark Sausalito houseboat floats on giant, spherical buoys of thick rusting steel. Rafts made from rusting steel barrels still support rustic structures. Quaint as they are, rust and rubber, of course, are no longer seen as environmentally sound choices.

No matter what the construction material, or its configuration, air is the medium that makes flotation happen. The greater the quantity of air enclosed in a single cham-

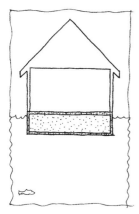

affects its movement: the lower its center of gravity, and the more uniform its weight distribution, the smoother the ride.

In terms of pure aesthetics, logs are the most pleasing means of buoyancy: Living folklore that defies both physics and biology. Many of the houses in Seattle and Portland, including the most elaborate new houses in this book, use the same material as the nineteenth-century logging camps drifting along the waterfronts of British Columbia and the Pacific Northwest: "old growth" cedar logs, four and five feet in diameter. Older houses sit on their original logs, estimated to be fifty to one hundred years old. Many newer houses use logs reclaimed from demolished houseboats, or purchased from brokers. Cedar logs last longer in water than in air, but as they gradually become waterlogged, houseboaters seldom replace them. Instead they, or a trained diver, simply add more flotation to the bottom of the raft, in the form of logs, plastic barrels, or Styrofoam blocks. The barrels are filled with water, positioned under the house, then pumped out. An older, successfully supported houseboat may rely on an inverted pyramid of logs and other materials, four or five courses deep. Because the well-preserved interior of old-growth cedar is prized as antique

ber, the riskier the ride. Floating dwellings usually float on hulls (one big air chamber) or platforms made of cellular material such as logs or Styrofoam (millions of minuscule air chambers).

Each type of flotation has its own style of sinking. Timing is an issue. When a hull springs a leak, water fills the airspace and drags it downward. (Watertight alarms, bulkheads, and automatic pumps reduce the potential damage.) Logs and Styrofoam simply deteriorate over time, usually with visible warnings: gradual lilting and sinking.

Houseboaters debate the topic of flotation most emotionally. There are two camps. One insists that the house should be attached to a rigid platform—a single block or basin of watertight material—and move with it (imperceptibly, if possible). Another camp claims that such houses bob ungracefully, like buoys, and they believe the flotation platform should be an assembly of multiple units—a raft of logs, for example—flexible enough to absorb the rolling and walloping motion of the waves without transferring it back to the frame above. The design of the structure sitting atop the flotation also

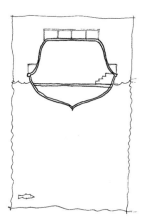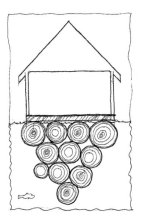

lumber, homeowners often joke that their wet logs below are more valuable and durable than the dry house above.

Thousands of years ago, the sight of floating reeds or logs probably inspired the first floating homes (boats). In our time, the arrival of reinforced concrete flotation (within the last couple decades) has inspired the powers that be—bankers, home insurers, real estate brokers, zoning officials, building inspectors, and other public officials—to begin treating floating houses like legitimate homes. Concrete makes for a modern foundation, and can be poured in factory conditions under the supervision of engineers and building inspectors. Moreover, concrete performs the best imitation of stone, the most respected "permanent" building material known to man.

Many of Sausalito's houseboats float on concrete barges made by Aquamaison Inc., founded twenty-five years ago by Ian Moody, in the former Arques shipyard where the first local houseboaters salvaged military debris. Moody built and branded his barges as consistent, dependable, and well-engineered products, something county officials could approve.

An Aquamaison barge looks just like your average basement: a concrete box with a stick-built top. But it works like a hull: its large, watertight, partially submerged volume forms usable space inside. A typical 16 by 36 feet. barge uses about two tons of reinforcing bars in the wall and floor slabs formed by the continuous pouring of concrete into the mold forms. After a few days, the forms

are removed and the exterior concrete sealed with two coats of cold tar epoxy coating. Built this way, the barge will last at least fifty years, Aquamaison estimates. The company also builds more expensive "thousand-year barges" by coating the steel re-bar (the Achilles' heel of underwater concrete) with rust-resistant epoxy.

Aquamaison builds its barges on a steel cradle, rolling on railroad tracks set into a concrete beach (slipway), to be then launched like ships right into the bay. The barge may be used for a retrofit (new flotation for a sinking houseboat), as flotation for a new houseboat being built elsewhere, or as a complete houseboat, with top and bottom designed and built by the company.

For retrofits—slipping new barges under deteriorating rafts or hulls—lifting is done by water, not by expensive marine cranes. First, Aquamaison workers build temporary, wood-framed supporting walls on top of the concrete barge walls. At high tide, the workers sink the new barge by filling it with water. They tow the old houseboat out of its slip and position it on top of the old barge. At low tide, the old houseboat sinks onto the temporary support walls of the new barge, and the water is then pumped out. Finally, the next high tide rises and floats the barge-topped-with-old-houseboat! The boat is then towed to the company's slipway, where the old flotation material is carefully extracted while the existing house is attached onto the new concrete barge.

In the late 1970s, Dan Wittenberg, a construction executive in Vancouver, had a revelation about his city, a waterfront capital unaware of its waterfront possibilities. Although Vancouver thrived on its maritime industries, history, and scenery, the water always seemed remote and inaccessible, buffered by steep sea walls and pleasure boat "parking lots," never bustling with people. Wittenberg

traveled down the North American coast looking for great coastal projects, but the trip only confirmed his conviction that waterfront development remained an unexplored, misunderstood frontier.

The more research he did, the more Wittenberg discovered missed opportunities around the world. Because the waterfront may be washed by rising and falling tidal waters, and often punished by nature's cyclical furies— storms, hurricanes, high winds, and turbulent waters— conventional wisdom suggests *not* building on certain areas (flood plains, for example), or *over-building* for worst case scenarios (building foundations deep in the mud, or cantilevering structures over the water or over floodable land).

Wittenberg's counter idea was brilliant. Think of water as real estate, he said. Why not expand the waterfront by creating a floating waterfront—complete with "roads," culture, commerce, and buoyant housing? Next, loosen up, and rethink the kind of structures the water might hold. Why not disconnect waterfront architecture from land and allow it to move with the water, for greater flexibility and safety at a lower expense. Wittenberg became a visionary in the truest sense: seeing big possibilities invisible to people who, much later, will call him a pioneer. He envisioned a grand scheme, then set to work constructing it piece by piece.

Yet two obstacles remained: flotation and bureaucracy. The waterfront was like disputed land in an unstable nation. Everyone wanted jurisdiction, but there was no choreography for making group decisions about the waterfront. Water agencies (which monitored everything from shipping lanes to snow goose migrations) were unfamiliar with construction. Water was foreign to land agencies, accustomed to treating the stuff as a hazard: to them rain and rivers translate into drainage, flooding, and storm water removal.

In Canada, as in the U.S., houseboats had a long history as alternative housing, floating under the radar of regulatory agencies. For floating buildings to be treated and welcomed as legal entities, first they needed to be insured and financed by reputable institutions. For financial institutions to consider them as assets, and not liabilities, maritime architecture needed to prove longevity. Wittenberg decided that the floating base would have to "outlive" the building it supported in order to win the confidence of financiers, investors, and inspectors. "Permanent flotation" was the answer. He devised an "unsinkable" means of flotation for buildings and their connective infrastructure. In 1981, he founded IMF (International Marine Floatation Systems, Inc.) to build flotation platforms using a proprietary design with patented details. "This is positive flotation. *Can't* sink," Wittenberg says. "Hulls are negative flotation. *Can* sink."

A "float home" platform looks like a solid concrete slab, about four feet deep, sized and engineered to fit the measurements of the weight and footprint of each custom-designed house. The platform is composed of expanded polystyrene encapsulated with structural concrete, and laced with an interlocking network of reinforcing bars. The platforms are insulated, but the surface of the concrete floor can also be cast with radiant heating systems. Space for electrical, plumbing, and storage features is also built into the platform as required by building codes and individual clients.

IMF claims the rigidity of the platform allows it to move well under different conditions. After the float home is built in the company's yard in Ladner, British Columbia, it is usually launched into the Fraser River. IMF houses have been towed by small boat as far south as Seattle, and as far north as Sullivan Bay. The houses are also light and flexible enough to travel by truck. Once houses reach their home slip, the low center of gravity allows for a gentle ride, IMF says.

IMF engineers are now collaborating with builders in the Netherlands to design and cast platforms for everything from floating homes to large floating districts. But Wittenberg hopes to win over his own continent before long.

OPPOSITE TOP *One Oregon houseboat combines boats, hot tub, and Buddha into religious expression: Be here now. Some Sausalito houseboats are like public art installations: collage, assemblage, bas-relief.* **OPPOSITE BOTTOM** *In Seattle, facades are garden walls hung with personal symbols. In Sausalito each Galilee dock mailbox has its own seascape.* **RIGHT** *Vibrating colors—in paint and mums—brighten a Vancouver marina.*

expression

Who can explain how the force fields of certain world cities affect behavior. Rome makes them drive faster and eat slower. Paris gets them to saunter aimlessly, sensually. Rio de Janeiro removes inhibitions.

Water communities can exert their own powerful influence. For some, perhaps the radical move off land frees them up to new possibilities. Or maybe water living attracts those for whom experimentation is pleasure, the more adventurous among us.

As water and shore belong to two separate realms—one inspiring artistic license, and the other rejecting it—houseboats have become public vehicles for exuberant personal expression. The phenomenon happens in paint, building materials, plant materials, and found objects, natural or unnatural. Worthwhile experiments often spill over into the "streets"—the shared dockways linking the houses into close-knit neighborhoods.

What is the profile of the houseboat designer? Recently, floating-home architects resemble bankers at a loft party, easy to spot with their clean-cut demeanor. The houses they build seem to be designed for land, unworthy of adaptation. The more interesting examples are those designed by architecturally untrained owners or design crews, who design with personal notions of utility and risk, so that the simplest floating box is as compelling as the fanciest pavilion. This is the quite different from land construction, where most architecturally designed houses offer far more theatrics.

EXPRESSION

68
—
69

Such sanguine improvisation has fueled houseboating from the start. Perhaps part of the do-it-yourself spirit comes from sailors and mariners, who only face the seas in boats they can repair.

When houseboats were relatively cheap and unregulated, they suited the bohemian ethos—jazz age, beatnik, or hippie. (Today, instead of ethos, we have *lifestyle*—the compulsion to use our hard-earned income to pay for home décor that spells "success.") Bohemians scaled down the size and expense of daily life in order to buy time to follow their spiritual pursuits. Instead of hating the job that paid for the things that they loved, they first loved their work—painting, writing, acting, crafts-making, exploring—and winged it from there. Making do was a time-honored bohemian practice, and still is. But finding affordable housing in urban dwellings has never been easy.

In contrast, the water has long been a bohemian refuge. In the 1970s, Sausalito houseboaters turned their resourcefulness into an anti-establishment art form: owner-assembled homes built without land costs, building permits, utility hook-ups or, ideally, store-bought building materials. From the local shipyards, they salvaged old hulls and topped them with millwork and

hardware rescued from demolition sites: old windows, doors, stained glass, brass hinges, and porcelain fixtures. On the waterfront, they maintained communal lumber piles. They inspired each other to reach new heights of funkiness—a kind of college-educated primitivism combining self-denial with self-expression.

"We were plugged into the back-to-the-land movement, except we were on the water," says Bob Kalloch, who, at seventy-eight, has lived on the Bay for almost forty years. "It was about the voluntary simplifying of your own life."

Although Kalloch's old houseboat stands out amidst the newer, more costly floating homes, neighbors treat him respectfully, as they would a living relic of the bohemian subculture that founded, and defended, water living in Sausalito.

Houseboat communities may be counter cultural—depending on their location—but there is an earnestness, even a fervor, common to all of them. People seem unafraid to flaunt the things that they enjoy. Like Sicilian-style passageways—with Madonnas set in neon-lit wall niches surrounded by soccer ads—houseboat docks offer wonderfully ironic juxtapositions, whether deliberate or accidental: satellite dishes and propane tanks; personal artifacts (a blackened wok, a decrepit boot) nailed to front doors as ersatz talismans; flotsam and jetsam flanked by real tribal masks; and impossibly beautiful dahlias bursting from rusted pots.

OPPOSITE TOP *In Sausalito, potting describes the dock's personality: Here, residents plant the dock area in front of their slip to form a linear garden. A Portland carpenter built a "Chinese" balustrade with 2x4s painted bright blue.* OPPOSITE BOTTOM *A pine forest, in plastic pots, grows in Seattle; hanging from the porch are privacy "curtains" of leaded glass windows. Near Vancouver, fiberglass artisans molded their own fiberglass experiment: an assembly of pre-fab panels; its patina resembles antique porcelain.*

These motifs defy suburban codes of decoration. Suburbanites use the same bland elements—fancy gates, light posts, topiary, and manicured hedges—to pull off the communal illusion of belonging to the landed gentry, as if from another time and place.

Houseboat people perform a very different show. They are more likely to represent where they have actually been (Tibet, Japan, or just a walk on the beach), than where they aspire to go. (Many aspire to stay where they are, right on the water.) They assemble what they admire and what they love to do, as they wish to entertain and delight their neighbors, not impress or placate them.

Received wisdom says that houseboat people can do a lot. They sail, fish, paint, raise vegetables, cultivate flowers, make furniture, build boats, weld sculpture, protect wildlife, raise exotic birds, and make wine—as, or in addition to, their varied professions and occupations. If anything, ingenuity, and not prestige, remains the language of competition.

Admittedly, some design elements are over-the-top: an elaborate water garden and fountain filled with plastic ducks; or wall reliefs playing on nautical kitsch (fishing nets, glass boats, boat fenders, brass bells); or beach-house sentimentality (shells, coral, driftwood, sea glass).

Some, on the other hand, are striking for their restraint: a few potted cacti, a driftwood branch, a lone bonsai pine. Political and religious statements are not uncommon: Tibetan prayer flags sewn into rooftop garlands, obscure amulets, and Buddhas of all sizes, and substances.

Some houseboats become outdoor galleries showing, or storing, the owner's work: A potter's huge vases crowding the porch like too many party guests, carved wooden totems, welded abstractions, etc. The most endearing, however, are the do-it-yourself assemblages, spontaneously Dada, occasionally sublime, made by those unaccustomed to making art. A planter made of a stovepipe stuck in a wheelbarrow proves that someone had a wonderful time surprising themselves, and the piece triggers vicarious surprise in anyone who discovers it. Good taste is beside the point.

Color is the most immediate surprise for houseboat visitors. They might feel like they've stepped off a plane and into a nation with a brighter sun, and greater intensity, like Cuba, or Mexico. One forgets how many colors are banned, by tacit agreement, for use on North American houses: Flamingo pink, lipstick red, safety yellow, Caribbean turquoise and lavender.

Houseboat owners misbehave further by combining taboo colors on a single facade. In Sausalito, Paul Hawken, the garden furnishings magnate, had his corrugated steel houseboat painted a bold pair of saturated colors. Neighborhood rumor says he took great pains to replicate the precise orange of the nearby Golden Gate bridge, and the exact blue of sail covers. But Hawken claims, "I just liked the colors."

Building materials and their detailing are also tools for experimentation. Residential docks can be wild versions of outdoor boat shows, where every slip holds a giant example of craftsmanship—antique or ultra modern—in materials as different as woods, plastics, metals, and textiles, all shaped for optimal display and seaworthiness. Houseboats combine unorthodox materials seldom used in land houses: mahogany; teak; bamboo; fiberglass; aluminum; and steel (stainless, galvanized, painted, or rusted. Today, the old salvaging aesthetic that embraced incongruous materials has been upgraded to a more "industrial" look—lots of steel and glass.

Le Corbusier, the French architect who loved the austerity ("the cold reason") of America's industrial structures, would have loved the ways in which Portland, Oregon's old boathouses and houseboats, roofed and sided in corrugated steel, share the riverbanks with factories made of the same materials. When the horizontal and vertical

stripes of a dockful of steel houseboats are reflected onto the rippling water, the effect can be dizzying. Portland locals have a special affection for galvanized steel as a material linked to their town's maritime history, but the spectacle of so many silvery, minimalist boxes on the mercurial water is a thrilling sight for even the most jaded avant-gardist.

Certain Seattle and Sausalito docks feel like period villages, preserving cedar shingling, which reached its creative pinnacle in the 1970s, when undulating siding and roofing was all the rage. Back then, houseboats resembled roofs without walls, as dramatic forms—A-frames, domes, and huge mansards—were covered in rough shingles.

Even the ugliest of materials—such as T-111, the common commercial plywood pressed to resemble costlier siding—are redeemed by colorful details: railings and balustrades made of rustic branches, high-tech cables, or colorful 2 x 4s. Houseboaters seldom hesitate to use building materials never actually meant for building. (Textiles work.) A Seattle couple used wool fringe to trim-line their fascia; it was originally made for desert use—to cover tents or camels—in Afghanistan. Elsewhere, silk scarves, fishing nets, flags, ropes, mats, and other weavings serve as summer walls, wind breaks, and sun shades. The end results look like the houseboats of Thailand, Vietnam, and China—layered with vibrant fabrics.

OPPOSITE *Deemed lurid on land, bright palettes—purple, pink, violet, turquoise—look correct on Seattle, Vancouver, Miami, and Key West houseboats.* **LEFT** *Outbuildings and satellite rooms—like this free-floating bedroom-on-buoys in Sausalito—make life more expansive.*

Among the most sublime floating landscapes in houseboat communities are the accidental gardens. Errant logs along the shores of the Fraser River, in British Columbia, bristle with Lilliputian fern thickets thriving on the soft wood and wet weather. Spontaneous as they are, with seeds distributed by birds, wind, and water, each garden shows the intricacy of a labor-intensive work of art, like a terrarium or bonsai. Sometimes "volunteer" gardens emerge from the exposed surfaces of a houseboat's flotation logs and merge with the cultivated gardens on deck. Water lilies form water gardens between some of Seattle's houseboats. But the most amazing feature of houseboat landscaping is the floating tree: A plant that starts out as a seedling, gradually sends roots right through the deck and into the water, and eventually entwines with the architecture and becomes an autonomous, hydroponic tree, sometimes dwarfing its host house, which begins to look like its planter box.

To the dedicated gardener, plants are art supplies, and gardens are works of color, form, and emotion. Sophisticated landscapes can reach heights of beauty lofty as any work of architecture or fine art. But gardening is probably the only art that makes amateurs look good, or at least poignant. Even the sight of a rangy eggplant, or a seed envelope skewered into a pot of soil, conveys hope.

Outbuildings—structures that look like mini-houseboats—also employ unlikely materials. Every marina has at least one adorable annex—a floating house-on-a-leash—that reveals something about the owner. The floating doghouse in Seattle suggests that the pet is fun, or the owner is cruel. A strange cubic garden of branches, built on a raft behind a floating house in Ladner, is a room-sized cage for a cockatoo beloved by its Canadian owner. In Portland, a utility shed fabricated in transparent, corrugated polycarbonate puts the owner's private storage on public display.

In addition to outbuildings, some houseboats use landscaped rafts (out-gardens?) for strategic purposes, like home expansion. In Portland, Ron Schmidt has three platforms: a large floating house, a backyard-sized deck, and a floating forest of bamboo used as a privacy hedge. On the deck, Schmidt installed a patch of artificial turf to help him drive used golf balls across the river.

OPPOSITE TOP *In Ladner, B.C., a backyard cockatoo aviary—built on a raft with studs and branches—doubles as garden. Accidental gardens decorate the log rafts of cabins on the St. John's River, Oregon.* **OPPOSITE BOTTOM** *Key West: No grass to mow at this floating grass shack where leisure reigns. Gardens form gateways to Seattle docks.*

OPPOSITE *Architectural plants, tall and spiky, give this Seattle houseboat its character; the "copper" siding is really faux-painted wood.* **RIGHT** *Log foundations double as planters for mosses and flowers.*

Houseboat docks show a range of gardening talent and intent as wide as their architectural accomplishments. No formulas, no perimeter or foundation plantings. Each container garden is a declaration of preference, designed from the pot up. The gardens express some other messages as well. There is no better measurement of neighborhood vibe than the number and personae of the gardens. The more plants, the merrier the place. The more fragile the plants, the more likely it is the owners are full-time residents, not weekend or seasonal visitors. Part-time houseboats, used for weekends or seasons, are emptier than full-time residences. (That explains why the marinas of tropical Florida may look barren compared Vancouver's.)

Houseboat residents often take it upon themselves to landscape the docks as well as theirs homes, creating two layers of gardens; both shade the houses, absorb noise, and perfume the air. The gardeners' largesse suggests that they like their neighbors well enough to fete them. And the permission given—to plant the public way—suggests that the neighbors like them back. Because container gardens require more maintenance than land plantings, greenery also performs an "eyes on the street" security service, suggesting that someone is home making the plants flourish. Indeed, lined up along the docks, cypress and cedar trees lend a particularly reassuring sentrylike presence.

Houseboat gardens rely on minimal structural support. Here too, the solutions are fascinating. A rock garden composed of cacti installed in rusted machine parts. A leather boot as a flower vase. Ancient oak wine barrels amid Costco containers and ceramics. Window boxes crafted like fine furniture, or salvaged furniture turned into window boxes.

Spiky cacti and smoother succulents are often displayed closer to eye level—on railings, ledges, and tables—than they would appear in normal gardens. Discovered on a houseboat, a desert garden may seem like a moonscape of foreign plants.

Some plants also need the houseboat to hold them up. And the houseboat architecture may depend on plants

The most famous floating landscapes may be the "floating gardens" of Dal Lake, home of Kashmiri "houseboat hotels." The gardens are rafts of tangled lake vegetation supporting crops of tomatoes, melons, and cucumbers. Boats can tow the crops around the lake—an alternative to truck farming!—since the crops' roots float, as well.

for its character. Well-trained or running wild, vines—trumpet, ivy, grape—go up trellises, or trail down balconies. Bromeliads grow from wooden pilings. Without the outrageous purple or orange wall behind it, a profusion of yellow marigolds or red mums would be less than startling. Without a layer of bougainvillea climbing it, a cedar latticework would be just a fence, not an explosion of fuchsia. Sometimes the plants take over. That's even better. When a jungle of pink cosmos engulfs a dour, old cabin, it is unclear if the owner is being rewarded for his toil, or invaded by seeds.

Kitchen gardens—some private, some communal—spice air already perfumed by pines, roses, and orange blossoms. In British Columbia and the Pacific Northwest potted rosemary and purple basil grow into robust shrubs, as if Miracle-Gro rained on the waterfront.

Disorder is another medium of expression on houseboats and docks. Although one person's chaos is another's order, disorder is usually a jumble, clutter, or disarray too complex to appear useful or lovely to most people. It is welcome in some places, but forbidden in others. When oceans wash tonnages of detritus onto the sands, beachcombers admire nature's bold messiness. But not everyone approves of a beachcomber's yard decorated with rescued jetsam. When houseboats are workplaces—homes to carpenters, mechanics, boat-builders, or artists—projects spill out into public view. Some residents are simply collectors of random objects. Some like to reinterpret junk by experimenting with context. And some just run of out room and park stuff outside the door where it can be as revealing, expressive, and random as art itself.

Order is expressive also. No one can move into a houseboat without submitting to the brutal process of self-editing. Land people often claim that they could live with less since they wear the same clothes, and use the same dishes, day after day. But houseboaters practice the art of leaner living. The proof is in their closets. Their home is not a museum of past lives and future aspirations, but an expression of who they are, pure and simple.

OPPOSITE *Bigger than a window box, this Seattle log foundation became a planter with cabin as garden ornament.* **LEFT** *Near Portland, a log raft becomes an accidental public garden. On water, native landscapes prove that chaos and spontaneity can look good.*

OPPOSITE *In Portland, Jantzen Beach marina seems like a Mediterranean sea village when it lights up at dark.* RIGHT *In Key West, city bikes beat the traffic.*

neighborhoods

A houseboat needs a home. It needs a *place* to stay and *permission* to stay there: a combination of solid footing and some pact, written or tacit, with the powers that be.

Houseboat jurisdiction is a jungle with a spongy mat of accumulated history, filled with impenetrable thickets of legal interpretations, overhung with a bureaucratic snarl of vines that stretch on endlessly.

In some places the jungle is dense enough to hide a houseboat in harmless tranquility. But in other places the jungle has been officially deemed an obstruction to progress and development. Because houseboats are hybrid by nature, defining them strains the patience of state and local policymakers. Thus it is easier to mow down the offending tangle, than to protect the biodiversity of houseboat communities.

Permission, like flotation, is a slippery fact of houseboating life. There are at least five assets to consider: the houseboat, the water, the land under the water, the dock, and the land at the end of the dock. Each of these assets may be described by paperwork or understandings of different sorts and tenures: direct ownership, condo, co-op, rental, and squatting. If a houseboat floats on a lake, all of the above-mentioned assets might be owned by the same entity. But waterways, saltwater or fresh, may include patterns of rights and sovereignty best explained by bubble diagrams. And on top of these rights may be "overlays" of special conditions like fishing rights, conservation areas, and navigation channels, each subject to change.

But as on land, the more you pay, the more permission you are likely to buy, and the longer and more secure your floating tenure may be. Unfortunately, permissions are becoming rarer each year, and the price keeps rising. A strong, protective framework of infrastructure and legal documentation makes a floating abode more secure, and more valuable, too.

But what makes a "good neighborhood"? On water, a good neighborhood is made up of a wide range of impassioned people, bound together by unspoken codes of live-and-let-live, and help-thy-neighbor. The mix of people determines the feel of the place; the feel of the place usually corresponds to the look of it. Generally, homogeneity—social or architectural—is not a seal of quality on the water.

Wherever they are, houseboat communities perform a remarkable feat: They are antidotes to their environment, whether urban or rural, surrounded by big buildings or big trees. Downtown, a household marina becomes a quiet neighborhood, or a weekend retreat. In the boon-

docks, a marina of similar proportions becomes a village, or urban node, inhabited by a dense mix of people, including cosmopolites.

The double dilemma of needing land plus water begs the question: Why not choose a real house on the waterfront? Once again, the answer is water. A real house needs to keep its distance to prevent flooding. There is a wide ring of land around many bodies of water—called different names in various places—that is unbuildable and unsailable. There are also huge swaths subject to cyclical flooding. Nature is notorious for punishing man's efforts to excavate and control his watery environment, but we are notorious for ignoring the message. Real construction digs down into the land (basements and footings) in order to stand up straight and buries its utilities (water, power, sewage). When nature wipes it away, man just rebuilds.

Floating architecture rises *with* the occasion, whether it be tide or storms. It provides a humbling and tentative place to live literally on the water. There is no need to reshape the terrain.

Marina infrastructure is to houseboats, what civic amenities are to houses: roads, sidewalks, driveways, entranceways, and landscaping. The design of these pieces determines who goes where, and how happy they are doing it. Each marina has a different *vibe*, as Californians like to say. The most harmonious villages may be the most tight-

Getting around the neighborhood and beyond is never boring by boat, transport that puts things in new perspectives and speeds—slower mostly. **OPPOSITE** *The marina on Mission Creek in China Basin, once an industrial zone of San Francisco.* **ABOVE** *Rowing past a marina in Marin County, California.* **FOLLOWING PAGES** *Seattle and Portland (left and right) If you love water, they say, you'll like the density of water-minded, but very miscellaneous, neighbors.*

ly packed, where the houseboats hug narrow docks on both sides and float remarkably close to each other. It could be coincidence, or an example of the power of urban design to engender human warmth.

In any case, houseboat civilization starts with the means of stopping: Unsecured, a floating house will float away. Anchored, or tied to an anchored buoy, it may reel around in the wind. The structure must be secured by tension—lines pulling in at least two directions—to come to a suitable standstill with minimal rolling and rocking.

In other words, a houseboat needs land. But it also needs enough depth to float during low tides or drought. (When houseboats hit bottom—and many do, daily—they risk tilting on uneven mud.)

A seawall offers the closest relationship of houseboat to land: curbside parking. If the water is deep enough, the houseboat sidles up to the wall, uses boat bumpers to protect both surfaces, and ties its bow and stern to hardware secured on land. In tidal areas, the boat is retied as

needed. A ramp, or gangway, bridges the gap between the house deck and the wall. Parisian *peniches* park parallel; some Dutch boats park head-in. In Miami, a small enclave of houseboats still clings to seawalls: years ago, the walls along Indian Creek and Miami River held large, linear houseboat neighborhoods.

Houseboats can also connect to shore, with ramps extended across shallow water between their doorways and dry land. Pilings—poles driven into the bottom—give the houseboats fixed mooring points. Early photographs of the Pacific Northwest show rough lumber shacks with gangplanks connecting them to land. Between Portland and the Pacific, houseboats along Oregon's John Day River recall the simplicity of those early structures, in greater quantity. The cabins, with toy-like proportions, are all sided in wood, roofed in corrugated steel, and weathered with different patinas. Though the cabins are far more private than most houseboats, they seem to be part of a snug fishing village on a remote island.

BELOW *Miami's houseboats—once numerous on the city's hospitable bays, canals, and Miami River—are disappearing. These 70s holdouts are moored on North Bay Island, an artificial isle in Biscayne Bay. The skyline is downtown Miami.* OPPOSITE *Rural, river houseboats in Oregon ramp directly to shore. Dock carts roll everything from car to home.*

DOCKS

Docks are the best way to organize houseboats into a neighborhood equipped with municipal services. Most residential docks are wooden boardwalks supported by timber or steel pilings. Concrete and aluminum also work as walking surfaces if they're textured for slip resistance. Walkways are layered with additional traction materials—non-slip runners, marine carpeting, rubber matting, etc.—which gives them an unusual quality of "indoorsiness" outdoors.

Docks are like faces, and there are many different dock configurations with a wide range of important proportions. The tiniest variables—the space between someone's eyes, for example—determine the difference between beauty and its opposite. The physiognomy of a place reveals its personality.

Traditionally, Seattle houseboats sit close to the water and tend to be tightly packed with slim air-spaces between houses, with front doors that open almost directly onto the narrow public walk-way that is the dock. Every inch counts.

Those four dimensions—distance from the living space to the water, spacing between units, space between the front door and the dock walkway, and width of the dock—are radically different in Sausalito and Marin County, where houseboats, floating higher over the water, are widely spaced along high, wide, fixed piers.

Seattle docks feel more like "college dorms," as one sixty-something resident described them, while Sausalito docks seem more like college campuses. The difference in scale alters lots of immeasurable qualities, like allegiance, cooperation, and trust.

OPPOSITE TOP *Seattle. Houseboats colonize unlikely places: under bridges, between factories, etc. Dock dimensions shape neighborhood life.* **OPPOSITE BOTTOM** *In Oregon, a short, river boat trip connects city to hinterland. In Seattle, front doors open right onto the narrow docks.* **LEFT** *Barnhill Marina and Boatyard overlooks downtown Oakland, CA, across a calm estuary.*

Mooring configurations—the patterns in which houseboats gang up—come in two varieties. *Clear-cut* moorages are arrangements that reveal themselves in one view, like a street lined with houses. *Mysterious* moorages are like convoluted old towns, windy or rectilinear, but not predictable. If there is logic to the design it will not be necessarily manifest to the visitor, and so the place seems larger than it is. Maybe the primal fear of getting lost creates that illusion.

The simplest clear-cut moorage diagram is a pier heading straight into the water, perpendicular to shore. Water supply, gas, and sewage lines can travel under the docks and branch off—via flexible connections, in some cases—into the houseboats. Electrical lines may also travel under the dock, overhead, or alongside.

Some docks, like piers, are fixed walkways on stilts. The houseboats may move a dozen feet up and down, but the walkways remain at the same height. In this configuration, the ramp connecting houseboat to dock often makes for a dramatic and steep trip. Floating docks follow the houseboat up and down, and put neighbors closer together by eliminating the vertical gap.

Single-loaded docks, like single-loaded corridors, line everyone up along one side only. Each houseboat gets a clear front and rear view, but fewer neighbors. Double-loaded docks temper the winds, and create the impression of a village street in pre-automobile times. The sensation of walking down this protective street—while floating on a river barreling along in another direction—is a reassuring, paradoxical thrill unique to living on water.

One of the most intriguing dock types is one that runs parallel to shore—single or double-loaded—out in deeper water. A walk down the ramp is peculiarly transporting for such a short trip: say, fifty to one hundred feet. It creates a duel sense of isolation and adventure, as if you're heading for a ship bound for exotic islands. In fact, the dock is a sort of island holding floating dwellings—which feel like smaller islands. "Island docks" also create two bodies of water to enjoy: a quiet inner canal, or moat, lying between dock and land (on the leeward side), and rougher water on the exposed "windward" side of the island.

Mysterious dock configurations are those with unpredictable site plans. Because they do not reveal themselves right away, visitors have a sense of discovery—or disorientation—as they follow the dockways.

One of the wide docks in the Waldo Point complex, near Sausalito, extends far into the bay, branching off into smaller docks, each reached by long ramps. Some of the branches end in dock platforms planted and furnished as common spaces for pods of two or three houseboats.

Sea Village—floating in the shallow marshes alongside the Intra-coastal waterway near Northfield, New Jersey—is also a configuration of long docks with short, asymmetrical branches. Composed of floating homes and houseboat vessels, the marina seems larger than its seventy-five slips.

At Point San Pablo, across the bay from Marin County, the marina is distinctive in several ways. The location defies definition; it is both urban and rural. Two lengths of breakwater—made of rip-rap layered on sunken ships—reach out into the calm water and enclose an oval of still calmer

OPPOSITE *On the St. John's, the river is the public way joining houseboats into a linear village of cabins resembling the earliest Western houseboats.* **LEFT** *At Barnhill Marina, a reclaimed cement-shipping wharf in Alameda, residents use old silos as storage lockers.*

OPPOSITE *Seattle. In the newest, non-funky marinas, houseboats are as big as laws allow; ambience is predictable.* **LEFT** *Roof decks are for watching the sky turn on.* **FOLLOWING PAGES** *San Francisco and Seattle. Left: The marina on Mission Creek before construction of "Mission Bay"—the huge, master-planned development that has saved it as "cultural amenity." Right: Seattle's cottage-size houseboats preserve the feel of original houseboat neighborhoods: cozy, not competitive.*

water. Floating docks branch off one of the arms of the breakwater, which doubles as a roadway. The Point is a former shipping area for produce, turned industrial harbor, turned movie set (a Chinese port for *Blood Alley* with John Wayne and Lauren Bacall); then an active, later inactive, naval outpost, the Point became a derelict marina, later renovated with a mix of sport fishing boats, floating homes, houseboats, and live-aboards. Ending a dead-end road, hidden by a series of hills, it has the hot microclimate, flora, and isolation of a tiny Baja port town, although it is in the middle of a megalopolis in Richmond, the Bay Area's city of industry, just over the hill.

No other kind of housing offers such strange and ironic contrasts. You can sit on a rustic cabin deck and contemplate the skyline of Seattle, Vancouver, South San Francisco, East San Francisco, Atlantic City, Manhattan, Miami, or Portland, and be interrupted by jumping fish. Or you can sit on your rooftop in a dense marina, amidst a dock party packed with one hundred people, and enjoy the starry sky dome ringed by the tropical hammocks of the Florida Keys, or the awesome mountain ranges of British Columbia or Oregon.

Wherever they are, and whatever they are attached to, houseboats keep residents well-grounded in a truth that becomes inescapable: all of us share the same habitat, and the closer we are to our environment, and our neighborhood, the better off all of us will be.

LEFT *Houseboat at the marina in Garrison Bite, Key West.* **RIGHT** *Signage on the community deck of Grant's Landing, a marina on the Fraser River, British Columbia, Canada.*

houseboat profiles

HOUSEBOAT PROFILES

*Granville Island residents Sylvia Rayner and Roger Dahlquist (shown dockside **RIGHT**) can float in a rooftop hot tub of their 12-ton floating house as home-made wine matures in deck-top barrels.*

49 degrees north

location: Sea Village, Vancouver, B.C.

owners: Roger Dahlquist & Sylvia Rayner

Go through the front door and you head straight for the water—the vertical panorama of blue waves topped by a blue skyline. Approaching from the other direction, via the water, you see the same double-height window with a different picture behind it: a view of domestic life afloat in a glass-fronted box.

The city is downtown Vancouver. The water is the saltwater channel called False Creek. And the address is Sea Village—the first legal floating home community in Canada—located on Granville Island, a rare example of arty city planning. (A cement plant, art school, theaters, and farmer's markets are part of the happy mix.)

This house inspires a strong emotion—curiosity—on both sides of the glass. From the outside, the place is mysterious: a minimalist oeuvre almost mistakable as ordinary industrial cargo in a city full of container ships. Inside, the owners can adjust their curiosity about the world outside by adjusting the house. When they close the tall, theatrical scrim (motorized shades), daily life can feel as private and serene as it does in a typical house. Once the shades rise, however, the place turns into a sort of maritime museum with a mini-IMAX of live kinetic scenery.

Day or night, the boat traffic and its hypnotic momentum never stop. Every few moments, something extraordinary passes by, at close range, with an eerie silence (the tight industrial sash seals out noise). The activity—a parade of vessels, mundane or exotic—is very urban. But without asphalt around it, there is none of the vibration, din, and dust that usually come with a mid-city view. The combination of urbanity and tranquility is quite amazing. The architecture of the house crystallizes the appeal of the place in its rustic yet polished design.

There are patterns: daily, weekly, monthly. Every day kayakers paddle inches away, some peering in as they glide by. Teams of dragon boats, oblivious to anything but speed, race past in much longer, skinnier boats (racing sculls).

The city's famously tiny ferries take commuters across the creek. And enormous barges, hauling excavation fill from downtown construction sites, travel back and forth, drawing low and high.

Every fair-weather weekend sailboats from the marina next door head out, en masse, to Gulf Islands. Paddle-wheelers, plying the creek on dinner cruises, no longer alarm the owners, who were once startled when a boat-load of tourists cruised by at close eye-level as the couple soaked, sans swimsuits, in their rooftop hot tub.

Among floating houses, or most houses for that matter, this one is unique in the way it delivers the drama outside without overwhelming the people inside. Skylights and window bays bring direct sun into the middle of both floors, and balance the intensity of the big windows. The design is essentially that of a townhouse made of two loft spaces. On the "ground floor" is a fluid expanse of living, dining, and cooking areas partitioned not by walls, but by deep-colored American cherry cabinetry. The upper floor is a continuous suite of sleeping, dressing, and working areas overlooking the double-height living area and the all-blue outdoors. Bathrooms, upper and lower, located on the land-side end of the house, are the only walled rooms.

The riser-less staircase was also pared down to its essential elements; the floating wood treads and rail seem to be an extension of the cabinetry. The staircase creates an intriguing, louvered view of the water as soon as you cross the threshold and enter the slate foyer—a second threshold where guests trade their shoes for Japanese slippers, and step down one riser onto a luxurious stretch of cherry Brazilian flooring that continues up to the water line.

Contradictions make this house fascinating and practical at the same time. It feels larger and grander than its floor space: 1,200 square feet. And the grandeur feels enveloping enough to be reassuring. In other words this is a rare example of a modernist house, uncompromised in concept or details, made comfortable.

How did they do it? More contradiction. The house is a no-nonsense, impersonal, industrial box—flat aluminum glazing (storefront windows), corrugated steel exterior, and plain plasterboard walls. The bland box lets in unfiltered views. But the structure holding up the box is a rough, Douglas fir timber structure, bolted to the floor with hefted steel bases. The rugged character of the wood, and those overscaled metal connectors, give the house a reassuring kind of stability.

OPPOSITE All who enter (through the front door, left) feel the IMAX effect—being immobilized by a moving picture larger than life. Two floors overlook the water, and its parade of boats, a through a double-height expanse of glass. A heavy timber structure of custom-cut Douglas fir created the clear spans and dramatic openness. The floor is Brazillian cherry. **RIGHT** *The sole bedroom is open to the staircase where nautical elements look modern, and vice-versa.*

Anyone can enjoy the house in two ways: as an architectonic abstraction, or as a subtle, evocative composition of everything nautical. It is a minimalist box that also looks like an homage to the plain metal boat sheds seen throughout the U.S. Northwest. The beam-and-column framework is a modernist way to build (no bearing walls). But the timbers also conjure up docks: the timber bays are slips; the columns are pilings; and the sleek units of hardwood cabinetry, sliding between the bays and past the rough timber, are the polished teak yachts.

The design process that brought these contradictions together was a collaboration between two architects and two owners. Roger Dahlquist, a telephone company technician, was living aboard his 48-foot sailboat, Song of Joy, moored in Coal Harbour (one of Vancouver's oldest safe harbors for houseboats and live-aboards.) That phase of his life ended when the marina expelled its residents. Next Dalquist and Sylvia Rayner decided to keep floating, but in a more elegant manner. The couple hired a Vancouver architect, Barry Downs, and continued to work with his associate Al Johnson as the process changed from design to collaborative "design-build."

"We took over the general contracting," Dahlquist says. "I was a laborer on the project because I like to build—and I had the time." The owners devised, and built, some of the furniture, hardware, and details. Rayner explains, "We're quite hands-on people."

Before starting construction, Dahlquist had spent two years fulfilling his dream of becoming a "lumber baron" by exporting Canadian White Spruce to Hokkaido for building traditional Japanese houses. Using his ability to find distinctive timber and move it, Dahlquist had a logger cut the Douglas Fir to their specifications and truck it to the building site.

The timber is heavy, but the tonnage—twelve for the whole house—is no problem for the barge underneath. It is a flotation platform of expanded polystyrene encased with reinforced concrete. The upper surface of the barge, the floor slab, was cast with a network of tubing inside to provide radiant heating via a water-to-water heat pump. The barge was made specifically for the house in British Columbia. The house was built directly on top of the flotation platform (minus the cabinetry and appliances), launched into the water, and then towed a few miles into its slip on False Creek.

Designing a house like this required a redesign of two lives. Scaling down from a townhouse, Rayner had to condense her life. Moving up from a sailboat, Dahlquist had to expand his. The compromise is a very graceful and revealing composition of what they love and what they need: luxuries positioned next to necessities.

Not everything is stored according to North American custom. "We have garages for our appliances," says Rayner, showing how seamlessly kitchen cabinets slide open and pull out. "But we don't have a garage for our car." (Sea Village provides one parking space per slip, in a parking lot nearby. The couple maintains three off-island lockers for chattel they have yet to edit.)

Designed by the owners, the house is full of hidden solutions to space dilemmas. Glass storage holds part of their collection of ceramic and glass art by regional artists. But the pieces do more than take up space. By rotating the selection the owners become curators, rediscovering what they have. The base of the glass case is a concealed horizontal pantry, for the good china. Two deep drawers slide out four feet on heavy rails of full-extension hardware.

Next to the sofas, a daybed flips open like a book, to become a double bed for overnight guests. The surrounding cabinetry hides the bed's legs, cushions, and a vacuum cleaner that hooks into a central vacuuming system. Seasoned by making sail covers for Dahlquist, Rayner sewed all the white canvas upholstery with a sewing machine she stores in the entry closet. Upstairs, the skylit closet is a kind of wardrobe-processing room with a

piggy-back washer mounted between cabinetry that holds carefully hung and folded clothing in blacks and reds.

Not everything, however, was worthy of storing inside the small living space. One outdoor wall opens and unfolds like a giant pantry to reveal a utility closet for tools and garden equipment. The garden is a collection of 110 potted plants, irrigated by a drip system, deployed around the house perimeter.

The wine cellar is actually in the "cellar." A concealed hatch, flush with the kitchen floor, opens up to a "hold" where Dahlquist stores wine of his own making. The "cellarette," cast into the concrete barge below water—level and originally designed to be water-cooled, nevertheless requires a bit of electricity to keep temperatures low enough. Each season, Dahlquist processes California grapes on Sea Village's floating docks, then ferments the juice on his floating deck in giant blue barrels. The finished wine does not languish. "We have people around a lot. They drop by and out comes the wine," Dahlquist says. "It's bloody pleasant."

And the wine is incredibly good. Maybe the quality has something to do with gentle agitation—of the wine, and its tasters, too.

OPPOSITE *The riser-less staircase has thin cable railings. The display, built of American cherry, stores good china while the glass case displays the owners' art collection of glassware and ceramics.*

blue millennium

location: Sausalito, California
owners: Tim Pierce & Karen Mulvany

They first met kayaking on a whitewater river trip. Now, Tim Pierce and Karen Mulvany, both forty-five, are floating full-time on Richardson Bay with their five-year-old daughter, Lauren Pierce.

"Actually this boat floats fifty per cent of the time," Pierce explains. "The tide is six feet on the average, and we go up and down." Down, in this case, means resting on the bottom during the lowest of low tides.

In 1997, Pierce and Mulvany bought a woodsy, 1975-vintage houseboat, and moved their offices into the three-level, 1,100-square-foot interior. He was a graphic designer; she was, and is, a financial consultant. After a few years of working off-shore and living off-water, they decided to trade places. They renovated the houseboat for family living, named it *Blue Millennium*, and moved aboard in 2001. Now both work on land: Mulvany in an office, and Pierce in a studio where he has switched to jewelry design.

Before its transformation, the houseboat was an amalgam of period clichés: cheesy drama, false economy, compulsive shingling, excessive wood, and inadequate light. It resembled a ski chalet because it was modeled after one. Previous owners built the boat using ready-made "ski chalet" blueprints featuring a steep, snow-shedding roof and tall shaft of après-ski living room overwhelmed by a wall of glass. They built the chalet onto an Aquamaison barge, and aimed the big window at the highest visible peak, Mt. Tamalpais.

The chalet-on-barge has two bedrooms and one bath on the lowest floor. The dock-level is the family area with an open kitchen, dining room, living room, and a bath next to the foyer. A mezzanine overlooks the living area and a large sweep of bayscape beyond; the family uses that level as a family office and guest quarters.

When Pierce and Mulvany decided to reclaim the house, they could not expand and renew the place with the usual modes of home improvement: adding new rooms, painting the old, buying new furniture. Changing the footprint was forbidden by local laws; painting over interior redwood paneling was taboo by local custom; and new furniture had nowhere to go.

Pierce decided instead to design and build the renovation himself, treating the house as an elegant piece of overscaled furniture, and ignoring its start as a miniaturized ski lodge manqué. In addition to the reconstruction, woodwork, and metalwork, Pierce also invented and built a "hydraulic rake," a powerful water gun that blasts away the "mud pads" that accumulate under the hull as boats ride the tides in shallow water.

Pierce and Mulvany aimed to change the character of their houseboat without altering the shape of the shell or its floor plan. Rough-hewn woods gave way to steel and hardwood cabinetry. Since the exterior shingles needed replacing, the owners searched for new materials with better performance. "We wanted color, fireproofing, no maintenance, light weight, and something I could install myself." The facade solution, ironically enough, was a product called "snow roofing": standing-seam steel available in a wild palette, including their chosen shade of changeable blue-gray violet.

Pierce towed the steel panels to the site using the floating deck, now moored at the back of the house, as a barge. While working on the steel roof that spans the entire facade with vertical seams, Pierce added two skylights to give the house a friendlier face, and to balance the northern light inside with some southern exposure. Adding direct sunlight warmed up the house considerably. The family finds it easy to adjust the ambient air temperature with simple mechanics. Using natural gas from a flexible pipeline serving the docks, the living room stove heats the largest volume of air, and a low r.p.m. central heating fan circulates it throughout the house. During the summer, the fan circulates the cool air, created by the cold water holding the concrete barge partially submerged. To expand the house without really expanding it, Pierce redesigned one of its prominent features, its railings. The house has lots of them: on the new front balcony, the mezzanine, two stories of stairway, and the rear decks, upper and lower. To elongate views of the water, Pierce eliminated as many barriers as possible. He surrounded the rear decks with transparent glass, and lined the mezzanine with translucent plastic. He also used railings as the boldest architectural element—a practical feature expressing his sculptural yen and resourcefulness. The curves of the front balcony and mezzanine stairs are electrical conduit, "a material designed for bending," Pierce says. He made a jig, bent the tubing, and arc-welded the wavy compositions himself.

Why does the interior feel so furniture-like? Pierce lined the dock-level floor with refined, beautifully detailed species of woods and grasses. He installed bamboo flooring, and designed and fabricated the kitchen cabinets and hall cabinetry in red birch accented with rosewoodlike African wood. He also designed and built some of the actual furniture in the spirit of the house, including the corrugated steel dining table. And he carved a Philippine mahogany frieze for the outer side of the kitchen cabinets. "The birds are cormorants," Pierce says. "But I took some artistic license."

The inspiration was the island bird sanctuary, visible (and often highly audible) from the living room's wall of glass. "Actually, it's just an old log raft that helps protect the houses from waves and floating debris," says Pierce. When the black and white birds line up in chorus formation, stretch out their wings, and vocalize en masse, the choreography looks like a Broadway musical. "It changes all the time, seasonally and throughout the day," Pierce says. "It's not just cormorants out there, but terns, sandpipers, and migratory birds returning year after year." The marina neighbors are like the bird populations: a great variety of water-loving travelers. Pierce says, "You find a wide range here—everyone from doctors to ex-hippies." Adversity, or at least its anticipation, is the tie that binds everyone into a loose community. "When storms come through, the pilings and ropes can break, so we're all watching out for each other."

The basic diagram of marina design also boosts neighborliness. "You're forced to talk to people on the dock," Pierce explains. "Because there's one way off and one way on."

burk/robbins house

location: Seattle, Washington
owners: Robert Burk & Blair Robbins

Their sparkly view of Seattle is unreal. Sea planes fly over a flock of seagulls coasting over a flotilla of sea kayakers splashing through an onslaught of white caps.

"It's a motion picture out there," says Blair Robbins, a filmmaker switching to a design practice she is undertaking inside her house and studio. "It's always changing."

In her new career, something between visual art and interior design, Robbins will project "Video Paintings" on the household walls of regular people—especially those who want the look of houseboat life (dancing light and shifting colors), minus the feel of rolling floors. Robbins films natural phenomena (cloud shadows, rain on water, etc.) on 16mm film, transfers the film onto video, edits it, and then projects the moving images onto walls. (Projector systems have gotten smaller and cheaper, she explains, showing an 8 by 3 inch box.)

But the "living paintings" are not the only experiment incubated in this houseboat. What began as a home improvement project became a three-year process, inspiring Robbins and her husband, Robert Burk, to transcend remodeling and go for sensory exploration in sound, movement, color, texture, and sleeping habits—all generated by their private design method. "We find something we love and build around that," says Robbins. They kept the frame of the house and its log raft, adding and subtracting as they went along.

"The whole house has fiber optics—about 600 pounds of wire in here," says Burk, who has done sound and lighting for Robbins' films and "collected" natural sounds with his wife over the years. The wiring will feed the projectors as well as the house-wide sound system.

"We will be able to move sound around the house," explains Burk, a geologist with an engineering background. "For example we might have night sounds in the bedroom, tapering off as we go to sleep. To keep the recorded night sounds *in*, and to keep real night sounds *out*, the bedroom walls are lined with inch-thick Tufcote—a barium-loaded vinyl product for sound abatement that looks like wetsuit neoprene, but feels like lead." Like the sound and video designs, the bedroom does not lend itself to photography. Painted dark blue, it is a low-lit compartment with a bed raised high over storage space. "We wanted a dark and cozy bedroom that didn't waste view space," Robbins explains.

The rest of the house glows with an intensity fueled by bright colors and reflective surfaces, lit by an east-facing wall of glass doors framing uninterrupted skyline. Tri-fold and bi-fold doors open one door at a time on hinges, or fold flat, accordion-style, to make the living room merge with the deck and feel like an open-air beach cabana shimmering with sun reflected off the water.

What appears to be plasterwork-on-stone—white, rounded ceilings and door arches—is really Sheetrock, curved to remind the couple of their Mediterranean trips. They dress accordingly. "When the winter sun comes straight into the kitchen and dining room I wear sunglasses and a sun hat," Robbins says. The windows are also tinted blue to cut the glare. (Is this Seattle or Santorini?)

During the day, when his glass desk reflects blue, water seems to flood Burk's office. At night, downtown gets projected into the dining room. "We used glass and steel to fit the glass and steel of the skyscrapers," Burk says. "The skyline would be a distraction if we didn't try to bring it into our house." City lights bounce off the water to the window or table.

Color here is not only bright but deep. Most of the walls were coated with Schreuder paint, a Dutch brand that is "more highly pigmented, won't fade in the sun, and is elastic enough to bridge cracks," Robbins says. The "mango" floors are bamboo, colored with a wash of the same paint, and sealed with a coating of pure urethane. For the interior window trim, they skipped primer, and rubbed the raw wood with paint.

OPPOSITE *Color and materials are experimental: stair treads are blue cowhide; stair risers are tanned carp skin; stair banister is nautical rope solidified with a fiberglass coating; "mango" floors are bamboo; antique wood doors are from Afghanistan.*

All windows of all rooms, but for bedroom and bath, frame the same mercurial panorama—shining skyline on sparkling water—for different domestic uses. **OPPOSITE** *Whether the owners barbeque out, dine in, or wash dishes, the view ennobles every task, including desk jobs.* **RIGHT** *Burk likes working on a glass pane at a glass wall where the reflections are unpredictable; office equipment appears to float.* **OPPOSITE BOTTOM LEFT** *Blue Bahia walls and a Murano glass tile floor give the shower a watery pattern. Sinks are glass, too.*

The strange, all-blue materials on the spiral staircase were also devised by Robbins and Burk. The treads are dyed cowhide. The risers are carp skin—yes, fish hide—farmed in Iowa and tanned in Canada. (They first saw the stuff on a hat band in Santa Fe.) The stair banister is thick nautical line (rope) solidified with a fiberglass coating.

Wildly colored stone appears in every room. Kitchen counters are wild-figured Blue Bahia from Brazil. The shower combines a Murano glass mosaic floor with Blue Bahia walls to make watery patterns. In the living room, a Danish fireplace-with-bake-oven, in nickel-plated steel, is insulated by slabs of ochre-travertine and blue granite. Robbins says the oven is great for cold, stormy nights. The bathroom is radiant too, with a heated towel rack, and heated floor of white marble tiles.

Nothing is more colorful than the house's exterior, a pulsating combination of blue and red-orange that helps make the building materials unrecognizable. In fact, what's real is fake, and vice versa. What seem to be blue ceramic shingles are actually all-natural siding, using three different widths of hand-chipped, painted cedar shakes. The orangey roof tiles—surely terra cotta, you think—are actually metal.

For experimentation, nothing beats a small house, Burk says. "We could buy expensive materials because we used small quantities in our small space." The reputation of the Burk/Robbins house looms large on the docks, however, especially during public house tours. Strangers gape. And the couple likes it that way.

OPPOSITE *Atmosphere is everything, not space.*
A wood stove heats the whole craft, and Christmas
lights are the only lamps. **RIGHT** *The assemblage of*
beloved stuff, mainly found and scrounged objects,
continues along the port side.

edwards house

location: Sausalito, California

owner: Robin Edwards

During the five years that Robin Edwards has been renting her one-bedroom, 10 by 35 feet boat in Sausalito, she eventually stopped trying to separate its real history from urban legend.

Unsolved mystery: Did Robin Williams really inhabit the craft while traveling the comedy circuit with its Irish owner? No, Williams told Edwards; he just partied there.

"This was a young landing craft personal carrier with a rocket hull, or something like that," she says. "It was built for the invasion planned for Japan if the A-bomb didn't work. These boats didn't flop down like other landing craft; they were supposed to bang into each other to make a dock. My boat, with its special hull, was supposed to be for the person in charge of the invasion."

"Next it became a 60s boat," explains Edwards, referring to the hippie era of "water squatters." "And later, a family of four lived here somehow. And I heard that a baby—now a grown man—was born back there in the bed." Edwards adds, "Boy, I thought I was downsizing."

Its current owner has talked about giving the boat as a gift to his tenant: "A retirement starter home," says Edwards, who is a collage artist and teacher. She imagines taking it to Oregon, or to New Mexico, on a flatbed truck. "I can see it on land, as a gypsy cottage."

Right now, sinking is not an issue for the wooden boat because it, like many other war-surplus-turned-hippie-houseboats, is supported on a concrete Aquamaison barge. However, keeping warm is problematic. "The boat is not insulated at all," says Edwards. She uses a wood stove, and lots of trips to the building supply store, for fuel. She laughs, "There are these million-dollar houses here, and I'm hauling in firewood all the time."

Within its three main spaces—octagonal bedroom, octagonal den, and kitchen/dining space—there is little room for furniture, let alone possessions. That suits Edwards. "Just about everything in here I found while walking the dog." She explains, "When people around here move, they don't take their old stuff to Goodwill, they just leave it down by the mailboxes, and it gets recycled." The castoffs are made more likable by seven sets of Christmas-tree lights used as her sole source of lighting.

"I also have the treasures that I've dragged around the world: a couple of jars of shards, sea urchins from Crete." Edwards says. "The things I loved then, are the things I love now."

go-getter

location: Sausalito, California
owner: Curtis Berlind

A retired Naval officer spent five years restoring this wooden logging boat, retired from the Pacific Northwest, to something of its former glory, a dignity much gentler than the old. It no longer guides log rafts down roiling rivers; in fact, it no longer moves at all. The Go-Getter retains its old name, but it basks in the sun, parallel to the dock in an outer slip, where its Richardson Bay exposure is wide and unhindered.

The boat's huge engine was removed and cleaned during the renovation, but not restored for duty. A modern cruising yacht this isn't. Getting the behemoth fueled up and underway would take a serious crew, and throw off plenty of fumes indoors and out. (The mighty smokestack behind the pilot house is a reminder of its industrial past.) The clean engine will be put back in place for the sake of authenticity and art. Polished up, it is a thing of muscular beauty.

A self-employed businessman, Curtis Berlind has lived and worked (using phone and computer) on the Go-Getter while working (using all possible tools) on the renovation. With the help of some paid labor, Berlind repaired and stripped all the wood; varnished the unpainted doors and windows; and painted the hull and pilot house a dignified combination of four colors: dark green, rust, yellow ochre, and white. He used sign painters' paint instead of standard marine coatings, to give the surface a better sheen and a longer life, he explains.

But for the sanitized engine, the interior is intact, complete with wooden floors sloped to shed seawater toward the stern. The entire hull has been cleared out and turned into a spacious, sloping office. The top floor of the pilot house, reached by ladder—where the captain once guided tons of log rafts traveling to sawmills and ports—is now an oval observation chamber with a 360-degree panoramic view of mountains and water. The main living quarters are on the middle floor. Towards the bow is a small, steeply sloped bedroom with its bed propped up level. The den has a steel-grate floor overlooking the engine room. The kitchen is minuscule yet original, with a zinc basin, tiny dining nook, and a massive stove. One can imagine drenched crew members, flapping around in storm gear, crowding the burners as their coffee boils.

Now coffee on the Go-Getter comes from a different place: the outdoors. Like a decorative fountain, an ornate espresso-maker, installed right outside the kitchen under an overhang, has turned the south-facing boat deck into a very domestic deck furnished with chairs and tables. This is the most spacious room of the boathouse, though it has one wall and no ceiling. Taking full advantage of Marin County's uncannily perfect climate, Berlind can adjust temperature, breeze, and privacy by pulling awnings over the southwest sides.

Baked by a steady sun, and sequestered in calm waters, the Go-Getter never had it so good. And now that the half-decade of labor is almost done, Berlind will soon enjoy the triumph of saving a hard-working vessel from the deep six.

OPPOSITE *Massive, enameled steel ovens and cast iron stove dominate the small kitchen where all corners are rounded. Dining is nautical: Lit by brass portholes, the eating nook has a walled table, grab bar, and filing drawers.* **LEFT** *Beyond the bathroom (with sliding door and compact corner sink), the curved bedroom overlooks the bow. Berlind's naval officer's jacket hangs from a porthole.*

OPPOSITE *Past archway and bathroom, the windowed bed compartment is reached by ladder. Décor is taxidermy, photos, and ceramics.* **RIGHT** *Neri shares a dock-garden, branched off the main dock, with these two boats.*

landing craft

location: Sausalito, California

owner: Susan Neri

Swimming would be the only way Susan Neri could get closer to the water and its wildlife. The distance between the water surface and the floor to her front porch is only twelve inches, and when she sits outside with friends they are soon joined by neighborhood ducks wading up the floating fowl ramps she built for them.

Neri's low-slung porch was originally designed for more strategic purposes. Although her vessel has all the charm of an antique riverboat imported at great expense from Amsterdam, it is actually a surplus World War II landing craft hull retrofitted with two canted side walls of salvaged, divided-lite windows.

The shallow-draft boat was engineered to slide onto foreign beaches, drop its ramp, and deliver American troops. At one end of the craft, two platforms open up on huge steel hinges, like the flaps of a cereal box. In its new incarnation, the cantilevered platforms stay open, forming a roof and parallel porch floor big enough to let a couple of guests—surrounded by clay pots holding poppies, geraniums, and pansies—bask in a perfect microclimate of southern exposure filtered by a rolling awning.

In size, shape, and headroom, the boat is no fancier than a mobile home: a rectangular tube of minimal space, 10 by 36 feet, lined with built-ins. But the character of the rescued war-vessel-as-cottage, combined with Neri's bright, offhand style of homemaking, make it an endearing place. The dancing light reflected off the water is dazzling. Tall, eight-pane wooden window sashes line up to enclose the space with symmetrical window-walls. For a house that is nearly transparent, it feels remarkably cozy somehow. At night, rolling window shades deliver complete privacy. The houseboat is composed of furniture, not rooms. You walk right into the kitchen (counters and open shelving on both walls); pass by the living room (banquettes on both sides); slide open a door to reveal the bathroom (tiny wooden sink, toilet, and shower); and find a very nautical, raised bed compartment just beyond.

What makes this compact tableau so intriguing? Maybe the strange workings of miniaturization: taking in an entire dwelling at a glance. It's no small achievement to compress life and work into 360 square feet, and to make that compression attractive requires a high level of art. Neri, an illustrator and graphic artist in her fifties, has edited out all but the essentials—a process most people avoid. After she figured out what she needed, she decided what she liked, a finer degree of filtering. The result is a revealing mix of lovably indispensable or indispensably lovable things.

All the kitchenware—exposed on the shelves or sitting on a red counter atop sea-foam green cabinets—is brightly colored: the colander is enameled red, pots are copper, everyday china is multicolored Hall brand ceramic. Bathroom clutter is condensed in baskets of different sizes. Multi-colored towels, rolled up like newspapers, fill the biggest baskets. The coziest retreat within this cozy retreat is the bed: a high niche with a low ceiling that spans the width of the boat. The bed feels sequestered,

but it's very easy to open it up to sunlight, fresh air, and panoramic marina views. Neri simply reaches up to open the skylight, or draws the curtains along the window that walls both the stern of the boat and one side of the bed. As houseboats go, Neri's is very responsive. It reacts immediately to anyone coming aboard (dips), to every boat cruising by (bobs), and most vigorously, to each passing storm (rolls). But Neri likes the ride and has learned to adapt.

Illustrating on a moving surface? "No problem," she says. "You move with it." Riding out storms? "When we get a bad one, some people will leave their boats and go to the library, or visit friends on land."

Neri also respects the fragility of this old boat—built to be tough, but not to be timeless. "You look into the bilge, see these huge bolts holding the hull together, and you get a sense of history, and how boats were made." Neri also gets a sense of suspense. "If one of those rusty bolts gives way, which could happen any minute, that's it. There's going to be a hole in the bottom." And then? An automatic bilge pump—one she checks every week—will kick in. If not? Neri remains untroubled: "Sausalito Fire Department would pump out the boat."

Neri explains how she came to enjoy precariousness as a way of life. "I moved here from a bigger houseboat I sold to pay my daughter's college tuition. It was 1,500 square feet, sat high off the water on a concrete hull, and it felt just like house."

Downsizing brought Neri the adventure she had been seeking all along: "I finally got a real sense of living on the water when I moved here."

OPPOSITE *The home is all here: one container divided by sliding doors. Seafoam green cabinets clash well with vintage housewares.*

lehigh valley 79

location: Brooklyn, New York

owners: David Sharps & Sarah Burd-Sharps

Cutting to the chase, David Sharps paid $500 for a massive old barge, rescued it from seven years of sunken oblivion at the base of the George Washington Bridge, pumped out 300 tons of mud, and spent two years getting the Lehigh Valley 79 up and floating—and, eventually, listed on the National Register of Historic Places. Built in 1914, before trucks and bridges took rail cargo across rivers, it is the last of the covered wooden railroad barges.

That happy ending was in 1998. A long story precedes that date. Another saga follows it. But the message of both is the same: find someone devoted to water, and they will show you an uncommon view of what living can be.

Twenty years ago, in Paris, Sharps learned about working on water as a student at the Jacques Lecoq school for actor-created movement theater (i.e., artful clowning), and as a skipper for a Parisian houseboat barge (peniche). He took fellow students out cruising the Seine, showed them the city from another perspective, and they performed on the boat. "The barge started to become a big part of everything," Sharps says.

But Paris was not the place where Sharps first met water. Before theater school, he had worked as a juggler in variety shows on cruise ships. "That got me out of the Appalachian Mountains and put me on the high seas, and that's where I fell in love with water."

After the Atlantic and the Seine, Sharps arrived on the Hudson River in 1984. He found a sorry boat, replaced it with a better barge, and headed to Manhattan-adjacent North Bergen, New Jersey, behind Palisades General Hospital. "It was the last surviving community of barge dwellers and they were moving us out to make way for new development," Sharps explains. "We wanted to be part of progress, not just a consequence of it. So we formed a museum to protect what we came to love about the water, to preserve the beauty of the river as a water highway carrying commerce and commuters." But after creating the non-profit, one-boat Hudson Waterfront Museum, he needed to find another barge to house it.

Enter Lehigh Valley 79, the sunken boat turned historic place. The renovation fueled an expanded plan: use the barge as a traveling "showboat" for public performances and educational waterfront programs—and, most optimistic of all, find a place to park. Hoboken was the barge's first "port of call." "We stayed for a summer, but we were a little too popular," Sharps says. "When our doors opened, one thousand people showed up." Asked to move on, Sharps became known as the "guy with the orphan barge."

Liberty State Park was the next safe harbor, until developers built a new condo-marina complex. Moorage fees for the big barge (30 by 90 feet and two stories tall) would have been exorbitant. Through the maritime grapevine, the source of former moorage locations, Sharps found a niche, Red Hook, in a receptive borough. "Brooklyn was a turning point. All of a sudden, we moved into a community—an underserved, impoverished area—that loved its waterfront and embraced us."

The barge, a.k.a. "The Waterfront Museum and Showboat Barge," was finally "put on the map," Sharps says. It worked as a floating classroom, exhibition space, and performance space for artists of many kinds. "The combina-

tion of the arts with a funky barge started bringing people out. We had time to raise funds, run a museum by day, and a showboat by night."

In 2000, however, tragedy struck. The barge was diagnosed with shipworm infestation. To survive, it had to be dry-docked and repaired—difficult since the city's few surviving shipyards were geared for metal, not wood. The closest dry dock was in Albany, the winter home of tugboats, and a repair facility owned by the New York State Canal Corporation. After $263,000 worth of renovations paid for by a myriad of government, corporate, and individual grants, the Waterfront Museum found a new moorage (its old pier having collapsed) in an industrial park, with riparian rights, between the Gowanus Canal and Gowanus Bay. Developer Greg O'Connell is the barge's waterfront angel.

The caretakers of the barge are David, his wife Sarah Burd-Sharps, and their children: Dalia, eleven years old, and Sophie, who is eight. Instead of a city park or suburban backyard, the kids have a wide-open seascape of water to explore. "In the summer, we've jumped off the barge to swim," says Burd-Sharps. "Our New York friends think we're crazy, but the EPA says the water is clean." (Atlantic Ocean water, that is, at the mouth of the Gowanus Canal). For drier exploring, the Sharps maintain a small sailboat and work boat to supplement car and subway.

Their adventure is not for the faint-hearted. Keeping the renovated barge hospitable is a relentless, physical challenge. "The barge is like a barn—not very airtight," says Burd-Sharps. (The hull is like huge log cabin of squared timber.) "So we use insulating boards to build an interior cabin in the winter, then take it apart again." Heat comes from a homemade system under the floorboards: Hot water, heated by two small oil burners, traveling through the kind of flexible hose used for radiant heating. "We can't heat the whole space that way, so we supplement it with a wood burning stove," Burd-Sharps says. "And that means hauling, drying, and chopping wood, of course."

In the WC is a #3 marine toilet emptied via five-gallon "honey buckets" (in marine speak) that Sharps hauls, periodically, to the local sewage treatment plant. Two on-board tanks each hold 150 and 250 gallons, respectively, of water delivered by hoses. A Sharps-devised system of pumps sends water up and down as needed. Land lines supply electricity. "It's pretty labor-intensive," says Burd-Sharps, an economist and chief of the United Nations Human Development Report Office. "But it's a beautiful space, and I believe in the mission David is working on. There are kids who've grown up right here in Red Hook, and have never seen the Statue of Liberty—until they come here."

For further information: www.waterfrontmuseum.org.

OPPOSITE *Part of the barge works as a public showboat theater for David Sharps and invited performance artists of all kinds. This is the stage.* **RIGHT** *Part of the barge works as a museum of waterfront history. The artifacts look like stage props and vice-versa.*

linde/li house

location: Vancouver, British Columbia
owners: Carey Linde & Dong Li

"It seemed like it would be interesting," says Carey Linde, an attorney who does not mince hyperboles. "But it turned out to be phenomenally interesting."

Ten years of living on a floating home in Sea Village—the houseboat marina overlooking downtown Vancouver from Granville Island—started out with an impromptu breakfast. One weekend, Linde was sailing up False Creek with some friends when another friend invited them into his houseboat. "That was the very house I ended up buying years later," Linde says.

But first, he learned more about the place from within, having been invited to social functions, and noticing that along with their gentle love for the water and their neighborly regard for each other, the residents "seemed to be having a hell of a good time."

In retrospect, Linde can review the mental mechanics of not making the leap offland and moving to Sea Village right away. "You think: It's probably safe to keep what you have," he explains. "But once you have a clue about something like this, take the risk, and push yourself into it, I think you find the reality is so much better than you ever expected."

The reality has been unfolding over the past ten years of Linde's time on the water. "The people living here have a sense of community, and I have not seen anything like it anywhere on the West Coast," says Linde, who grew up in a small Vermont town where generations of families kept neighborliness intact. The only place that compares in his memory is a self-contained village, home to the First Nations Haida tribe in the Queen Charlotte Islands, where Linde lived in the early 1970s.

What also amazes Linde is the way nature envelops everyone all the time. "I didn't have that feeling about nature in the days when I lived right on a beach," he says. "But now that I do, I find it hard to consider living on the land again—in a fixed spot. Here the water is always moving. Maybe the movement makes you feel tied into the process of things. It's like Mother Earth breathing up and down." Linde adds, "I have an undulating front lawn!"

The wildlife has quickly grown in size and diversity over the years, as the creek has become cleaner. "Now Dungeness crabs come to spawn," Linde says. "And there's always been herring in the spring, huge swans, geese, ducks, river otters, raccoons, beavers, and an occasional harbor seal coming right in, looking for food." At night, as the city calms down, and the water absorbs sound, the Village seems even more rustic: "It's very quiet here, and we're smack in the middle of the city."

Granville Island, just across the saltwater channel from Vancouver's financial district, is a former industrial enclave revamped as a cultural village mixed with a few industrial neighbors, such as the concrete plant next to Sea Village. "Living on the island is like being off-wing in a major theater production," Linde says. "There's always something happening, something open until late at night. There are theaters, restaurants, galleries, art school, markets, tennis courts . . . And the selfish aspect is that those fourteen of us fortunate enough to live in Sea Village are the only people who live on Granville Island."

Commuting is absurdly easy for Linde. He takes a toylike water taxi across the creek and arrives at his office within twenty minutes, door-to-door. As a flight attendant for Cathay Air, Linde's wife, Dong Li, often travels thousands more miles in her day, but Vancouver Airport is not far away.

Their floating home was built by a hands-on family in 1976, according to the spirit of the day, ubiquitous woodsiness. The post-and-beam structure was oversized for drama, and the family sided the remaining inside surfaces with rough cedar. The exterior is ship-lapped, painted "spruce or hemlock," forming a perfect backdrop for a built-in, linear forest of cedar trees, Japanese maples, bamboo, and wisteria. The flotation platform, cast in Richmond, British Columbia, is a reinforced concrete barge loaded with Styrofoam.

"Everything is eight-sided: the barge, the building on top, the rooms, even the bed headboards," Linde explains. "I think it had something to do with Egyptian numerology."

In their travels to China, including Dong Li's birthplace near Tibet, the couple has brought back furniture and mementos for their "Chinese room." The house is big enough to fit most of the objects, but small enough so it "stops you from spending money on collectibles," Linde says. As for the great wall of books, "They're ballast," explains Linde. "No, really."

OPPOSITE TOP AND BOTTOM *Inside, the original post-and-beam structure was paneled horizontally, in rough cedar. The present owners added a casual collection of furniture and mementoes, in carved woods and bronze, brought back from their travels to Dong Li's birthplace, China. As for the great wall of books in the tall living room, Linde explains: "They're ballast."* RIGHT *Elevating a bed over drawers saves space in the nautical tradition.*

lindner house

location: Portland, Oregon
owner: Gary Lindner

"We're a boring people now—passive," says Gary Lindner. "We want to be entertained, but we don't want to work at it."

Lindner, who grew up surfing in California and now lives in Jantzen Beach, the "Venice Beach of Portland houseboat marinas," decided to work at his "huge affinity for water." He bought a small floating home moored to a large floating deck-as-backyard, holding a hot tub on top and three boats alongside (one kayak and two powerboats).

"In Portland, people don't really know that houseboats exist. There's no local coverage," says Lindner. "Coming here from California, I see them in a different light. Someday people will realize this is Malibu."

Lindner renovated his one-bedroom houseboat, added a deck and hot tub, and under the tub's potential 400-gallon load of water, extra Styrofoam blocks beneath the log flotation raft. "The house is one hundred percent wood: All cedar inside and out. No drywall," says Lindner, who likes the product Oregon grows. (He moved north to work for an architectural millwork firm.)

Jantzen Beach is a condo complex of houseboats served by a gated parking lot and all utilities. The land was once an amusement park partially owned by the swimsuit magnate. "I own the water surface of my 28 by 60 foot moorage, but the Port of Portland owns the water," Lindner explains. "The moorage fees—for services, maintenance, and upkeep of wetlands—are like condo fees. Except that everyone pays the same monthly fees whatever the size of their house."

Along the quiet slough that forks off the Columbia River, houseboats share the water with pleasure craft and small working boats. On the other side of Hayden Island, the waterscape expands into a huge maritime diorama of giant Chinese container ships anchored mid-river (with names like "Glorious Prospects"), container ports with awesome steel arms lined in menacing rows, and ship-building companies.

The natural scenery is also dynamic. "There are so many things happening down here," Lindner says. "Last night the sky was orange out there. We get some great fogs and mists because we have a different climate down here. The river stays warmer than land." Lindner watches birds mark the seasonal changes. Swallow families return to his bird houses. Loons come back to the slough for winter, and recommence their eating patterns: "They dive for ten minutes, and then pop up again." Blue herons take their turns using his deck when he disappears.

The most dramatic of nature's cyclical events is the flooding that Portland expects every dozen years or so. "In 1996, the river rose twenty feet or more. The nails in the pilings mark the high water line," Lindner says. "We almost needed tugboats." (The tugs would have pushed against the houses to keep them from leaving their moorages if the pilings loosened or gave way.) Some of Portland's very tall pilings now have extensions to keep them above future flood water.

"We are very, very dependent here. If your house breaks loose, I'm in big trouble," Lindner says. It's that grim possibility that helps make dock mates into real neighbors. "There's a spirit here that doesn't live anywhere in subdivisions."

OPPOSITE *At twilight, the Londahls can head up the Multnomah Channel, towards Portland restaurants, in their 1929 Dodge Watercar.* FAR RIGHT *The mahogany floor of the boat garage sinks into the water, and the boat backs into the river.*

londahl house

location: Portland, Oregon

owners: Kris & Kym Londahl

"Boats pull up to the house, a foot away, and people peer right into the reflective glass. They don't know we can see them, and they can't see us," says Kym Londahl. "We don't chase them away, but sometimes we just open the door and say hi. It's a shock that people really live here."

In a city with more houseboats than anywhere in North America, the Londahl house is remarkable for several measurable reasons: width, expense, and weight. Its nickname, the *Stone Houseboat*, refers to the 410,000 pounds of exotic masonry floating on a log raft. The roof is concrete tile. Idaho mica is the glittery cut stone facing the facade and the big deck columns in back. Inside are smooth horizontal expanses of "Rainforest" marble from India mimicking the wild, flaming patterns of red gumwood from Louisiana swamps. (Kris Londahl knows about materials and their detailing; he started out as a glazier, before moving on to develop software for auto glass installation.)

This is the biggest, by far, of sixteen floating homes in a co-op on the Multnomah Channel. Its 4,000 square feet of bi-level floor area are supported by a series of steel stringers, laid across a 70 by 62 foot "float foundation" of old growth cedar logs. Roller arms under the house help it glide up and down the pilings as the river level changes. "But the house can't move back and forth," Kris Londahl says.

The floating home co-op and boat marina is hidden from view off a weedy side road, only ten miles from Portland. The dock runs parallel to the shore, leaving a canal-width waterway—between the floating houses and land—providing "curbside" parking for the homeowners' boats. Across the water is a separate world still more remote from the city than their waterfront: it is Sauvie Island, a 24-mile-long preserve of farmland and game refuge, linked to their shore by a single bridge—the one nearly overhead.

The Londahl house includes features Frank Lloyd Wright might have designed for Midwest American prairies: low, hipped roof; horizontal stripes of ganged windows and overlapped cedar siding; and great expanses of elegant wood decking and porches overlooking a serene stretch of water (à la Zen temples). In fact, the Londahls like Wright, and so does their architect, Mike Barklay. (In the 1920s, Wright designed houseboats of his own: several semi-Asian "barges" proposed for the Lake Tahoe Summer Colony.)

The couple asked Barklay for plenty of party space, in and out. "We wanted large decks and patios for different seasons," Kym Londahl says. Their entertaining gravitates outdoors, she explains. The couple has hosted "huge parties" on their deck to watch the Christmas parade of lighted boats. Londahl likes "ladies' pool parties" with margaritas. "We float around in inner tubes and plastic mattresses," she says. "But we have to stay tied to the dock since the current is strong."

At night, the glass waterside facade of the house becomes a lantern of orange light reflected by the channel. Patio floods illuminate the double-height columns. Underwater floods, lining the deck, give the water an eerie glow, as they remind guests not to fall overboard.

Sometimes, the Londahls take friends out to dinner in their boat, an exquisite 1929 Dodge *Watercar*, with a deck

and hull of African mahogany. Like most suburban vehicles, the *Watercar* is housed in an attached garage, with automatic garage door next to the kitchen. But the ritual is unique. Between trips, the powerboat rests in an exalted state of dry-dock on posts mounted in mahogany floorboards milled from the timber's denser inside core. But when Kris Londahl presses a button, the boat—and its floor—ease down into the water. Guests hop into the floating boat and drive off.

Since each of the co-op slips comes with its own two-story, studio-over-garage, the Londahls have land parking, too. Their two garages house only four of their six cars, however: a Chevelle, Bel-Air, Austin Healy, and Corvette made between 1955 and 1970, plus a new Lexus and Land Rover for normal driving.

Their current motor yacht stays in Annapolis, M.D., during the summer, and in the Caribbean in winter. Their new, 74-foot cruising yacht being built in Taiwan will be delivered to Miami. But their Portland deck is equipped with brass cleats huge enough to hold it.

According to Kris Londahl the next frontier is not a bigger houseboat, or a bigger boat, but more time on the water. "Kym is a city girl and I'm trying to convert her to a water girl," Kris says. "The next level is *living* on a boat."

By *boat*, Londahl means one of those ocean-going vessels designed to keep moving.

OPPOSITE TOP *Heavy with mica, marble, and a concrete tile roof, the 200-ton house is moored to a floating dock, parallel to the riverbank, which rides up and down on extra-tall pilings. Filling two slips, the structure floats on a deep raft of old growth cedar logs topped with steel stringers.* **OPPOSITE BOTTOM LEFT** *A skylighted staircase rises past the double-height living room to two large bedroom suites.* **OPPOSITE BOTTOM RIGHT** *Kris and Kim Londahl deckside in their Dodge Watercar.*

morris house

location: Lake Union, Washington

owners: Gene Morris & Margaret Thomas

Experience may be the answer. The question is this: How can a family of three live gracefully in 900 square feet?

Living in houseboats since 1970, Seattle architect Gene Morris had already learned the art of condensing personal space for the expansive privilege of living on water. (You change habits and chuck household stuff to get more living out of less house.) In 1985, he added design experience to his floating expertise, and collaborated with an interior designer—his wife Margaret Thomas—to build a cottage on Lake Union for themselves and Julia, the baby.

How does the architecture fare now that Julia is sixteen? With one bathroom and two bedrooms, her place may be one-quarter the size of a medium-size American house with multiple baths, but it rates high in two categories of teenage esteem: style and freedom.

"My friends think it's cool," Julia says. Her dock neighborhood is an intricate village of flowery gardens and toy houses, and her living room overlooks a marina of sailboats coming and going. Her very private bedroom, on the third level of the four-level house, is reached by an intriguing set of stairs.

As for independence, Julia had an extremely hip means of transportation—named *Philomene*—long before she reached driving age. Docked at the rear deck, is a 16-foot, 1959 Tolycraft, a "roustabout" powerboat with the wonderful wood-and-chromed metal detailing of a vintage Chevy. Morris bought it in a used car lot.

"Julia loves driving Philomene around the lake," says Morris, who explains that there is no age limit for boating. As for family fun, every couple of weeks they dine out on their boat at sunset, in the middle of the lake. And they all like to kayak and "jump off the end of the dock and float around in life jackets."

The Morris family did not set out to build a brand new house. They bought an old houseboat, floating on 75-year-old cedar logs, and aimed to rescue and reuse as much as they could. Like most Seattle houseboaters, they rejuvenated their base with some new logs and plastic barrels strapped to the bottom. But a closer look at the rest of the house revealed that little else was salvageable. Most went to the dump, though they saved the original, pot-bellied, Howard overdraft stove, a cast-iron beauty with nickel-plated parts. The old stove is the main source of heat, helped out by electric space heating.

The cedar-shingled cottage is designed to take full advantage of its slip location. The more public faces of the house—side walls and dock-side facade—use glass sparingly. But at the back of the house, facing the sailboat marina (usually empty at night), a double-height living room frames the scenery in large, arched wooden windows custom-made by a local window company. Glass living-room doors open onto the deck for family dinners or entertaining.

The small master bedroom, on the uppermost level, borrows the marina view and sense of spaciousness by overlooking the living room like a balcony. The tall headboard, with its tiny twin reading lamps, is not a massive chunk of wood, but an armoire open in the back. While her husband works mostly from his office, Thomas works at home at a desk in the living room, and in the bedroom at an ingenious drafting table made of two tabletops sliding out of the wall cabinetry on full-extension hardware, like drawers.

The couple was also clever in making uncommon uses of standard construction materials. The exposed, living-room ceiling is made of laminated 2 x 4s. The ceiling is paneled in hemlock. And the floor is 4 by 6 inch double tongue-and-groove "car decking," sturdy enough for garages.

The next question is this: When Julia leaves home, after a lifetime on water, will she choose a non-floating college, or enroll in Semester at Sea?

OPPOSITE *The headboard doubles as armoire in the bed-sized bedroom—overlooking the living room—where roof rafters meet with tent-like geometry.*
LEFT *No license is required to drive Philomene, the Morris' 1959 Tolycraft roustabout powerboat docked at their deck.*

mudlark

location: Sausalito, California
owner: Jenette Foster

From the outside, it looks more like a playhouse than a dwelling, but inside, the Mudlark, moored in Sausalito's Galilee Harbor co-op marina, feels remarkably livable for its 270 square feet. Charm is the quality that makes the place seem more expansive than it is. Economy inspired the resourcefulness that makes the charm compelling.

Its owner, Jenette Foster, was an artist working in downtown Sausalito, when she first saw the Mudlark, a neglected cabin built on a flat-bottom redwood barge. It was a mess leaking from the top, bottom, and from its windows, too. But Foster saw potential; overpaid for it; then asked Tony Marciante, a harbormaster, to help her gut and rebuild the 9 by 30 foot interior. "We worked side by side for months," Foster says.

Exhaustive salvaging was the art that gave this boat its redeeming appeal. The waterfront is rife with terrific junk, Foster explains. She amassed doors, leaded glass windows, antique lighting fixtures, wood trim, brass hardware for the kitchen cabinets, and just enough vintage redwood tongue-and-groove paneling to line the interior walls. Every scrap of building material, and every fixture, has a provenance Foster recalls with pride. The prized fixtures—miniature cast-iron stove with rusty flue, knobby chrome kitchen faucet, and flophouse-style three-burner range with porcelain knobs—were all acquired for nothing, or close to it, from dumpsters, docks, salvage yards, and flea markets. For the kitchen counter, Foster collected stone and tile refuse, and mortared and grouted the shards into a pique-assiette composition à la Antonio Gaudi.

There is no furniture. But built-in cabinetry forms a perfectly workable kitchen, a "salon" (with a wall-to-wall window seat sofa under a homemade plastic skylight), and an upstairs sleeping loft with wall-to-wall mattress. There is no plumbing, per se. The houseboat hooks up to running water via an exterior faucet that connects to a marina hose. But the waterless WC contains no more than a portable potty, emptied in intervals, at a marina holding tank.

The all-wood, all-funk interior might have looked a bit sinister if Foster had left the materials—all dark and patinated—in their authentic state of decay. By "whitewashing" all the woodwork, with paint thinned down to reveal some of the colors and textures underneath, Foster unified and brightened the tiny space. She prettified the exterior by coating not only the clapboard siding, but also the metal roofing, with a glossy white paint trimmed with powder blue fascias. For her efforts, fellow residents of this, the most defiantly bohemian houseboat marina in town, dubbed Foster the Martha Stewart of Galilee. In 2002, Foster decided to move away and put her boat up for sale. In Marin County, where the meanest of water-view condos and bungalows cost millions, her pied-à-l'eau was not high. Asking price: $35,000.

OPPOSITE *The window seat—lit by a Plexiglas skylight and found sash—forms most of the living room.* **LEFT** *Storage cabinets double as compact stairs to the bed loft.*

potato chip

location: Sausalito, California

owners: Alexander Rose & Gwendolyn Johnson

"In the harbor here it's known as the Potato Chip," says the Chip's owner Alexander Rose. "But its real name is the Guy Lombardo, and I don't know why."

Rose bought the houseboat four years ago from Keith London, head of the model shop at George Lucas' company, Industrial Light and Magic. London, who had lived on the strange craft for twenty years, gently repairing and remodeling it, told Rose that two Berkeley architecture students had built the Lombardo in the 1970s as a graduate thesis project. And that's exactly what it looks like: too sophisticated to be folk art, too primitive to be contracted.

The boat was an experiment in form and materials that works in mysterious ways on the Bay. Its curves are magnified by the geographic waviness all around. Docked in the Galilee Harbor, below a steep cascade of Sausalito hills, just under a distant panorama of Mt. Tamalpais and on top of an open expanse of water, it is surrounded by backdrops that change shape with the shifting light. As the rippling water reflects in canted windows, it animates the curves.

Because the construction is hip and naïve in equal parts, the boat demands an extra dose of attention to figure out whether the builders were ingenious, or just winged it with great success. The inspiration seems to have started with the hull, salvaged from one of the surplus steel lifeboats made for the World War II Liberty ships built in town. Seen from the side, the wooden top mimics the lines of the metal. The window panels are stripes of opaque fiberglass and clear Plexiglas set flush with the edge of the roof (and resembling a slice of fruit).

"This was always one of my favorite boats when I was growing up. I like the Pringle roof shape-a hyperbolic parabola," says Rose, who was raised in two Sausalito tugboats. (One sank; the other, next door, is still the home of his mother, a Marin County supervisor.)

The swooping roof is a thin construction of redwood boards topped with tarpaper and roofing compound. "I heard they built it on forms and lifted it up," Rose says. "It's in tension." The roof plane—potato-chip thin—is slightly twisted to give it extra strength.

Inside, the curves create optical illusions. "It's one room, 13 by 36 feet, that feels much bigger than it is," says Rose, who lives comfortably in the loft-like space with his friend Gwendolyn Johnson. "I think it's the amorphous roof, with the strong slope, and the fact that all the walls are windows, which makes it impossible for your brain to grasp what's really going on in the space. You have nothing to compare it to. And so it doesn't feel as small as it should."

The amorphous quality of his dwelling suits Rose's job. As executive director of Longnow, a San Francisco foundation, his mission is to encourage long-term thinking for a better society. (Long meaning very long: 10,000 years.)

Although the dock is being upgraded, its amenities are simple. Electricity comes from "funky extension cords" on the dock; water, from water hoses. WCs on land are shared by the co-op, but Rose's boat has a bathroom sink, and a small corner shower "with about six different 3D curves in redwood, plywood, and tile," Rose says. A pellet stove heats his space; propane cooks the food. Keith London built the kitchen and bath cabinets in recycled teak. Sausalito artist Timothy Rose, Alexander's father, made the three mobiles dangling from the ceiling.

One of the great cultural conveniences about houseboats, one learns, is that mobiles move all by themselves, all of the time. Even when the boat feels stable. Alexander Calder would have loved the Guy Lombardo.

POTATO CHIP

160

161

OPPOSITE *Gwendolyn Johnson reclines undisturbed by the curving roof, canted planes, and constant movement. A pointy kitchen and an angled bathroom (sans plumbing) are tucked into bow and stern.*

OPPOSITE *Inspired by the modest tradition of Seattle's cabin houseboats, this one conceals some drama inside. Custom windows are equipped with motorized exterior shades.* RIGHT *A porthole in the very dry basement, the concrete flotation system, reveals a visitor's legs.*

strobl house

location: Seattle, Washington
owner: Heinz Strobl

His reputation preceded him. But it was the wrong one.

A few years ago, the word on one Seattle co-op dock was that Heinz Strobl, a young, Austrian-born Microsoft "retiree" who bought one of the old houseboats, aimed to destroy it and build anew. The low-key neighborhood feared gentrification—not wealth, per se, but its pushy expression.

Certainly, they believed, the newcomer's replacement would fill the allowable zoning envelope, and tower over their cottages with an architecture of reproachful dimensions.

The neighbors' fears seemed to be confirmed when they heard Strobl had hired a respected architect (Gene Morris) and marine engineer (Craig Goring, who built the foundation, though not the upper part of the house). The worry escalated when they learned that the hyper-designed, towable floating home was being built in a for-

eign country (Canada) without a traditional cedar log raft, and that the new-fangled flotation base—one that resembled a concrete basement—had an underwater porthole for watching fish.

And for this, the neighbors would have to surrender their homes. "It was an upsetting process because it meant all the houseboats had to be taken out to make way for his, and all this had to happen in one day," says one longtime dock resident. "In the old days, you wouldn't think twice about dragging them out. But that was back when they weren't worth anything." The neighbor adds, "And nobody *knew* Heinz back then."

Another resident explains, "People here are protective of their neighbors' right to be funky. Next to Strobl's slip, Dave—an articulate but low-tech (no phone) former social worker—lives in a house of no apparent architecture, with just corrugated steel roof planes visible above a thick assemblage of found objects (which happen to be Dave's passion). Could the extreme houses co-exist happily?

STROBL HOUSE

162

163

On the big day, when Strobl bought food for everyone as a house-moving celebration, there was much to learn. Strobl found his dockmates to be warm and friendly, especially when all houses returned intact; dockmates discovered that Heinz was a sweet and modest man with a playful sense of humor.

Strobl's invading edifice turned out to be a warm and sociable cottage reflecting local houseboat history, in playful patterns of stained cedar shingling and eyebrow-shaped arches of metal roof covering a quirky form. As for the old house displaced by the new one, Strobl had intended to remodel it all along, but was thwarted by its height—too tall for the code's limit of eighteen feet. But Strobl saved the old house after all, by donating it to Seattle's Center for Wooden Boats.

Since one side of the cottage faces sideways, towards maximum sun, with two levels of windowed walls and a large deck, Dave's place is framed in a new context: now the installation seems more editorial (private décor as free speech?) than ever before. Visitors like it and so does Strobl. The single-story cabin is so low, it lets in plenty of light.

Architect Gene Morris says that Strobl's requirements were simple: maximum daylight, optimal views. Plus one submarine window. "It's hard to explain why," Strobl says. "But water intrigues me."

Morris used a roof deck to get a panoramic of the sky-line. Inside, the two-story house holds a surprising view, reached via an elegant foyer with a stainless steel-railed staircase. At the top is a grand living room, arched over by bold, criss-crossing steel roof trusses. Strobl gets a commanding view—of the outdoors and his indoors—from the shiplike railing. He can look down into a small-er living area that joins dining room and kitchen, or out across the village of houseboats beyond his deck. When Strobl needs to adjust the exposure—for shade or privacy—he presses a button and tall, motorized shades drop down, like movie screens, outside the windows. The large cedar deck is a floating dock for kayaks and swim-mers; its cutout curve fits the shape of his future boat.

The building of the "basement" flotation was a project unto itself. The architect asked the Vancouver firm IMF (International Marine Flotation Systems) to build the flotation, the first concrete platform in the neighborhood of log rafts. But IMF had staked its reputation on build-ing "positive" flotation in reinforced concrete and expanded polystyrene—basically, thick, unsinkable plat-forms—definitely not on hollow hulls with submerged windows.

"IMF said they had never built a house that *could* sink. And the marine engineer said he had never built a boat that *couldn't* sink," Strobl laughs. "But this basement is drier than most people's basements." (There are bilge pumps on duty in case of breach.)

For the moment, choosing the room's purpose is more important. Wine cellar or billiards den? Would move-ment wreck a table game or enhance it? Strobl is enter-taining ideas. For the moment, the empty concrete room, with its single window of blue-green lake, is mesmeriz-ing. Nothing large swims by, but there is suspense in waiting for something that does.

OPPOSITE TOP *The arched, steel roof recalls 19th century houseboats. The patterned shingle siding is stained cedar with galvanized steel detailing. Steel trusses create an open living room overlooking kitchen, dining, and lots of Lake Union.* **OPPOSITE BOTTOM** *Leading from entry to living room, the stairs feature stainless-steel railings. In the kitchen, the post-and-beam structure, "stone" tile floors, and granite counters spare no weight.*

the taj mahal

location: Sausalito, California
owner: undisclosed

For thirty years, Bay Area guidebooks have mentioned the alluring and inaccessibly white Taj Mahal in many languages, and it remains a legend in its own time. It's there, yet it's not there. The secrecy is provocative—if you can find the thing, which you're not supposed to. It is private and perplexing. If this mini-Taj is not a marble cenotaph built by a Mughal emperor for his beautiful wife, is it a film set, a branch of Skull and Bones, a cruise-up Masonic lodge, or a themed yacht club? Luminous in a beautiful coating of fresh paint, it is indistinguishable, at a distance, from white marble. But at close range, the mini-monument seems more like huge wedding cake, Islamic-style, sided by sugar latticework and creamy frosting.

If you locate the onion domes peeking above masts of the private marina, where regiments of stately sailboats look like warships protecting the Taj from outsiders; if you bypass the No Trespassing signs (occasionally hung by marina management), and walk down the long dock flanked by boats pointing their prows like bayonets; and if you come face-to-face with the Taj archway—blocked by a chain holding a discreet sign, "Private Residence"—then you would confront the taunting riddle: If this is a house, where's the house? (In marinas, one should do the right thing, and ask permission to enter.) More pointedly: Where is the front door? Doorbell? Windows? Security signs (omnipresent in California)? Potted plants? Any signs of life at all? The dock entrance is completely obscured by elaborate, layered wood screens. The Bay facade is faced with expanses of glass, bringing light and views of passing sailboats into an inner courtyard.

TAJ MAHAL

Local live-aboard sailors confirm that the house—built on a concrete hull in the 1970s—and the 40-foot sailboat docked nearby are the weekend retreats of a local family.

The Taj is fascinating for its contradictions. Unlike most houseboats, moored in dense villages, bristling with balconies, decks, and windows jutting into public view (and flaunting personal taste), this one floats in a parking lot of empty leisure boats, sealed and discreet, intriguing as a limousine with blackened windows. It is both formal and funny, intimidating and toylike—a landmark that bobs on the water like elaborate bath toy.

How does it float? Shah Jahan, builder of the original Taj Mahal in 1631, would have probably floated his if he could. He liked water reflections. In Agra, the monument stands on a platform built right on the Yamuna riverbank; its entrance arch is the culmination of a long reflecting pool.

Color, and its changeability, is another feature this white, wooden houseboat shares with its white marble precursor. In India, they say the Taj Mahal is changeable—pink in the morning, blue-white in the evening, and golden in the moonlight—just like the moods of a woman.

LEFT *The entrance faces the dock, with a mysterious screened porch, Mughal-style.*
OPPOSITE *A concrete foundation seems to levitate the wood house above the water.*

OPPOSITE *From the 1970s, Sausalito's heyday of funky, carpenter-designed experiments, this vintage assembly is an antique train car split in two, mounted on a concrete foundation, and enveloped by house and decks.*
RIGHT *In the submarine bedroom, pillows lean against the waterline. Bed curtains are fringed hemp rope.*

train wreck

location: Sausalito, California
owners: Henry & Renee Baer

"We had no intention of buying a houseboat," says Dr. Henry Baer, a man with the impeccable diction of an upstanding, land-owning citizen. "We were just looking for Mill Valley property, came here, and it was love at first sight. The best move we ever made."

That impulse purchase was no ordinary houseboat, but a unique work of extreme carpentry, named Train Wreck, that is, a built approximation of a rail car crashing into a house and staying put. Inside is a split Pullman car from the Northern Pacific Railway containing two rooms.

The Baers discovered the *Wreck* when a real estate agent directed them to the Marin County houseboat marinas and explained the math: Assuming the legend is true, and no unit in the Sausalito hills costs under a million dollars, then houseboats—starting at about $250,000 and topping out at one million—cost one quarter the price of standard houses.

The houseboat benefits included those for which Marin County is famously expensive: "Better weather and more natural beauty than in other parts of the Bay Area." But soon Baer, a physician, and his wife Renee, an interior designer, discovered invisible "fringe benefits" incalculable in real estate numbers, and impossible to describe without piety. Baer struggles to avoid clichés, then gives up: "It's like a village here. With a sense of family. I've never experienced it anywhere else."

Meanwhile, just beyond the neighbor's unpretentious house lies a marina full of spectacular and functionally pretentious sailboats, some equipped to cross oceans with crews. "I like to sit here and watch those boats not leaving," says Baer. "I'd say half of them have never left their berths."

Train Wreck took eight years to build. In 1976, Keith Emons acquired an 1889 North Pacific Railway Pullman car—with its intricate mahogany paneling and brass fixtures and hardware completely intact—sliced the box in two, splayed the pieces apart as if hinged on one side, and lowered the gaping car onto a hollow concrete barge. Emons built the rest of the house around and atop the car, exposing some of it to the outside and enveloping the remainder. As you walk around the exterior balconies and decks, through the mazelike interior, pieces of the train car appear and disappear in a disorienting series of peek-a-boo vignettes.

The front door opens right onto the lovingly restored dining room section of the Pullman car. Exit the dining car/dining room, enter the living room, and you see the outsides of both segments of train car. The joint—connecting the two segments with no more than a few inches of metal—is an unnerving example of architectural tension, a detail that creates a strange kind of physical empathy. The metal seems to act like a tendon keeping two broken limbs from flying apart. Emons used the rupture as an archway to the staircase leading to all three levels of the house.

Upstairs is a study filled with sunlight and views over the water. You reach the bottom level by walking down the

Within their "village" the Baers have found plenty of urbanity. The distinctly non-suburban mix of people respects the unwritten law of city living, "Live and let live," Baer explains. "It is an eclectic group. On one dock you may have a winery owner, a drug dealer, an architect, a welfare person, a handyman, and various felons, too. But we're all equal in our own way."

Baer points to the inscrutable dwelling next door. "That neighbor, for example, is in the Guinness book," Baer says. "He builds ocean-going rowing shells, and he can go forty miles on eighteen-foot-high swells." Surrounded by skinny boats longer than itself, the house is grander than a shack, but hardly the sort of architectural neighbor most physicians seek. Heroic architecture, however, does not necessarily engender heroes, as Baer sees it.

LEFT *The house unites eclectic pieces collected on trips.* **RIGHT** *Roofed over, the train car appears to be traveling through the house.*

stairs, right under the eerie black Pullman chassis where the working parts are exposed like the flip side of a horseshoe crab. Because the lower level is formed by the walls and floors of the Aquamaison barge, its floor lies several feet below the water surface. (The draft of the barge depends on the weight of the house and contents.) The master bedroom suite occupies the entire floor with a luxurious bathroom, a giant walk-in closet, and a bedroom barely larger than the bed itself. The Baers like the quiet privacy of sleeping and bathing in the dark "underwater" part of the house.

In effect, the Baer's houseboat is a celebration of travel by train and airplane. Assembled from the antique car, and filled with antique artifacts airlifted back from the couple's travels through Asia, the boat contains some very intense collisions of cultures and architectural parts, all within 1,900 square feet.

Although the Train Wreck does fit into both the salvage and assemblage traditions of Sausalito houseboat construction—its aesthetic is more complex: homage, perhaps, to two aesthetic movements rising during the early 1970s—conceptual art and historic preservation. Back then Robert Matta-Clark was slicing old, abandoned houses in two, photographing the fissures, and creating sculpture as faux vandalism. Meanwhile, preservationists were performing controversial acts, too: halting demolitions, and advocating the expensive repair of outdated buildings.

Emons performed the violent act of splitting the antique Pullman, but he also spent those years of gentle, painstaking craftsmanship using ingenious detailing, making the defunct train into a comfortable home. This is a strange, emotional mix of shrill art and sentimental craft, but the fusion works.

And it floats.

OPPOSITE *The sink, with overhead wine compartment, lies within the train car, but the rest of the kitchen breaks out of the box, into the living room.* **ABOVE** *Lined with closets and clerestory windows, the embedded Pullman car/hallway leads to a whistlestop-style balcony.*

trott/christiansen house

location: Sausalito, California

owners: Susan Trott & Roy Christiansen

"Water has always been important to me," says Susan Trott, a novelist and artist in her sixties. She met her Norwegian husband, Roy Christiansen, on a freighter bound for Argentina. "Roy was the chief engineer on the ship, and I was running off to sea."

Trott got swept up into another water adventure when she took a tour of floating homes. At the time she was living comfortably in a Mill Valley house-on-land. "I wasn't even looking for a houseboat—or a house, for that matter. But after seeing a house for sale on that tour, I ran home, ran back, and put down a deposit," Trott says. "Of course, everyone said I was crazy."

From the inside, however, Trott's way of living appears perfectly serene and reasonable. One of the simplest of Aquamaison's designs—both the concrete hull and wood-framed house were built by the local firm—the Trott/Christiansen house is a boxy, two-story volume with bedrooms and work areas downstairs, and a lofty living/dining area at dock level. The pastel paint and furniture tints not only intensify the sunlight, but they dramatize the deep blue landscape, spanning the whole living room, behind glass doors. Their balcony overlooks a grand expanse of blue water defined by houseboats, aligned like townhouses, around a village green. "We call that the Lagoon," says Trott. The blue-on-blue landscape,

bordered by the purple curves of Mt. Tamalpais, incalculably expands the real dimensions of the house. "The big sky was an unexpected benefit."

A powerboat moored at the floating dock moored to the Trott/Christiansen house allows the couple to add still more borrowed territory to daily life. They often cruise up the Sacramento River Delta or picnic on nearby Angel Island, a national park that looks like a forest moored mid-Bay. Occasionally, their house acts like a boat. "When storms come, it's fun to rock and roll," Trott says. "Otherwise, this houseboat is so stable, you forget you're floating."

When they return from exploring the semi-wilderness of the Bay region, the couple enjoys the urbanity of the marina. So does the indigenous wildlife, Trott says. "I've seen raccoons strolling two by two down the docks. In the lagoon there are seals and diving birds of all kind."

As for other citizens: "There is a marvelous variety of people here; it's like a village. There are progressive dinners at Christmas time, and parking lot yard sales in the summer," Trott says. "I'm close to my family and friends in Mill Valley—I can walk there—but I feel like I've moved away. It's a perfect life."

RIGHT *Barb and Will Watkins run a riverside bed and breakfast offering one floating cottage.*
OPPOSITE *Moored on the banks of Fraser River, the Waterlily is a little room with an awesome view.*

waterlily

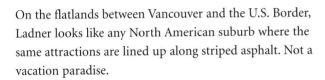

location: Vancouver, British Columbia
owners: Will & Barb Watkins

On the flatlands between Vancouver and the U.S. Border, Ladner looks like any North American suburb where the same attractions are lined up along striped asphalt. Not a vacation paradise.

But crossing Ladner, in search of River Run Cottages at the mouth of the mighty Fraser River, makes contrast part of the payoff. Beyond the malls are beautiful fields of fruits and vegetables tended by First Nation farmers, and fisheries lined up along a steep embankment paralleling the road. No water, though.

As it turns out, the banks are dikes, holding the edge of the tidal river. Beyond the rise is a surprise landscape of water meeting a grand backdrop of pines, mountains, and sky. It's a milder version of rounding a pass and finding Shangri-la spread out below.

When the tide is lowest, and the ramp steepest, the houseboat called Waterlily looks impossibly small from above—too tight for the coziest off-season weekend. (The tide sends the Waterlily up and down, fifteen feet, twice a day.) But as soon as you walk inside and down a couple

steps, the Waterlily expands like an optical illusion performing its untraceable tricks. How did it grow right before your eyes? Expectations may explain the magic. This houseboat is neither house nor boat; more like a huge piece of inhabitable wooden furniture, detailed and hand-crafted with sincerity and whimsy, intuitable right away as a labor of love.

Although its builders—a young couple that hand-crafted the pieces while they lived in the shell—parted ways after a couple years, their optimism was not wasted. It is rediscovered by a constant stream of admirers—new ones each weekend. The proof is in the guestbook on the bookshelf.

The Waterlily is the only buoyant unit among River Run Cottages, a small bed and breakfast owned by Will and Barb Watkins. They live in a larger houseboat sharing the dock with the Waterlily, which they bought from earlier owners.

This houseboat is not really a house, but one tall room layered with usable levels and devoid of movable furniture. The beautifully varnished loft bed, stretched over the bathroom, is reached by stair ladder. Each riser is carved with an anchor and drilled with a thumb pull; it conceals a shelf of storage. The bathroom's normal size makes it seem grandiose compared to the rest of the cabin. Over the compact, marine-sized bathtub, a brass porthole holds a bubbling fish tank that doubles as "skylight" and white-noise machine for privacy in close quarters. The living room furniture is a banquette raised on stairs, overlooking the river through a high band of windows. On the "ground" floor, an efficiency kitchen and a wood stove provide the other comforts.

The real attraction is the way the small craft delivers river life. Sea birds arrive on deck, salmon below; kayakers paddle past sunsets. But nothing compares to the sight of a working boat cruising past late at night—no sound, no wake—with a fisherman, his face illuminated by a single light bulb, cleaning his catch on deck.

Vancouver may be twenty minutes away, but part of Ladner remains as it has been for a long time—a true fishing town. Of course, you would never know this unless you were on the water, at night, looking out the window of a houseboat.

OPPOSITE *Two steps above the "kitchen," a banquette forms the living room/library/guest room.*
RIGHT *A stairladder—of concealed shelves opened by thumb pulls—leads to a loft bed with low ceiling.*
TOP *The Waterlily's owners live in a floating house next door; its kitchen opens onto the river.*

yellow ferry

location: Sausalito, California

owners: Chris Tellis & Isabella Kirkland

The Yellow Ferry moored at the end of the "Yellow Ferry dock" has had a remarkably long history, both as a working vessel (a Seattle ferry) and as local landmark famous for its size, color, and antique features: a wooden paddlewheel and a tall smokestack secured by cables.

The Ferry is also remarkable for another kind of longevity. Three generations of the Tellis family have lived aboard. Chris Tellis grew up on the houseboat his family bought in 1958. (Tellis is the founder of Antenna Audio, the company producing audio tours for museums around the world, Louvre included; his wife is the painter Isabella Kirkland.) Now the Tellises are raising their eleven-year-old son, Nate, on the water too.

Nate Tellis, who was born on the Yellow Ferry and has never lived in a "real house," is articulate on the subject of houseboat living. His home "feels just like a big house, but if you look out the window you see absolutely nothing but expanses of water." In a storm, the view may start "rolling from side to side," but "you hardly even feel it," he claims. Nate appreciates the water from afar, unlike his

father. "My dad swims in it most mornings with a boogie board and wetsuit." (His father confirms, "I'm in it all the time.") Father and son have traveled together on the water using their legal "floating island": a 16 by 18 foot raft, with motor attached, registered as a vessel. It's versatile, Chris says. "We've camped out in the middle of the bay, and gone caroling by float, too."

Sausalito marinas have changed since the elder Tellis' childhood: "This used to be a legitimate artists' community," he remembers. "Now it's the bourgeoisification of the waterfront—but it's still good." There is still plenty of neighborliness, maintained in part by the pedestrian-only network of docks. "Mainly, it's running into folks," Tellis explains. "That's the organic process of close encounters."

The beauty of the Bay seascape remains unchanged by time and real estate. "The water is like a kinetic meadow with sky reflected. "It can be a dazzling blue, golden, or gray and sinister," says Tellis, describing how living on water colors daily life. "The house comes alive."

Work from Attika Architekten, Amsterdam, show-casing imaginative vision for new floating com-munitites **OPPOSITE** *Rendering for FarWest, a commercial building.* **RIGHT** *Study for floating neighborhoods in the new IJburg development district (reclaimed water) near Amsterdam's center.*

future

LIMBO

Late in the last century, North America finally decreed clean water and clean air to be the inalienable rights of all citizens. Next, we expanded our global economy and sped the cleansing. Industries disappeared along with their effluents and emissions; containerized and reduced to fewer ports, shipping shrank.

The results are cleaner waterways rolling past abandoned land: ghost landscapes dotted with factories, warehouses, parking lots, train yards, docks; and piers disassembled by weather and weeds, devolving into wilderness. It is an amazing sight. But the waterfront acreage is so wide and remote it takes a plane or a boat trip to get the full picture.

Lately, these places have been called brownfields, lands of unknown toxicity languishing as developers and government agencies decide how to launder them for new uses. On a continent where greenfields seem endless, brownfields constitute a new kind of fraught real estate. Location? Superb. Much of it borders protected waterways slicing through magnificent cities. Liabilities? Untold.

Even if billions of dollars were freed up to transform the land for greener uses, big plans take a decade or two to flourish. Meanwhile, millions of waterfront acres are stuck in limbo, locked into post-industrial indecision, neglect, or turmoil, zoned for activities long-gone.

An alternative to limbo is short-term use. And what better interim use than residential marinas—mobile by nature, designed for being towed away if and when better options arrive twenty months, or twenty years, later?

NEW RESIDENTIAL MARINAS

Think of post-industrial waterfronts as a new frontier ready for colonization by pioneers—those impassioned people with high standards for adventure and lower requirements for normalcy. (Replacing Western frontiersman are artists taming messy urban frontiers.)

Working together in public-private partnerships, developers and city officials could do the following. Seal a parcel of industrial land with pavement and planting: build access roads, parking, storage, and maybe a few amenities for marina visitors. Build an infrastructure of permanent or moveable docks. Size the slips for a combination of floating homes, houseboats, live-aboard boats, pleasure boats, and perhaps working boats too (fishing, eco-tourism, sailing schools).

Governments could collect revenue from personal property taxes, permits, moorage fees, etc. They could also provide affordable housing in mixed-income neighborhoods, monitor and clean the environment, promote outdoor recreation, reduce sprawl, and uphold historic preservation—duties governments are supposed to embrace.

The best houseboat communities are compact, socially mixed, and inexpensive to build. (It's the dearth of slips that keeps prices high.) Houseboaters are potential stewards of the environment. Like wildlife, they prefer quiet, calm, no-wake zones with swimmable waters. They can alert officials to emergencies and emerging problems, and help to provide a sense of security for other boats on the water. They are also potential protectors of nautical heritage, the next frontier worthy of historic preservation.

OFF-THE-GRID LIVING

In the old industrial age we were bad. We enslaved rivers, sliced off mountains, squandered coal, gas, and oil. Now we have a chance to be good.

A new era has begun just as invisibly as the old one has left. Soon, we will have cheap and clean energy from the sun, wind, and newfangled batteries. We will no longer have to pipe in power or pipe out wastes, making a mess both at intake and output. At last, we have figured out how to use natural resources without using them up.

ABOVE LEFT *Sketch for the huge IJburg housing development, where some waterways are reserved for floating homes.* **ABOVE** *"Waterhouse" in Oosterbeek, 2003.* **OPPOSITE** *Sketch of Waterrijk in Almere: site plan for a flood-prone part of town.*

Now we can unhook our homes and live anywhere. Not only can we can live on water, but we can live there more cleanly and virtuously than we could on land. Water living is "living lightly," bulldozing neither land nor vegetation. We know how to turn human waste into usable compost. We can transform available water (rain, river, salt, and wastewater) into water for drinking or household use. We can make enough power to send some back to the grid.

OFF-THE-GRID HOUSEBOAT DESIGN

Boatabode is the name of the high/low-tech water dwelling I'm designing for an off-the-grid (O.T.G.) neighborhood of the future.

Boatabode is small house celebrating a great moment in history: We're free. A slew of newly affordable inventions have finally made it possible to live a clean, self-sufficient modern life unplugged and unplumbed to one place. The idea is to pack the best new methods and machines into one house and to set it adrift (or at least afloat), free from all conduits, pipes, and cables.

Using photovoltaic cells on its outside skin, wind turbines on its frame, and fuel cells in its concrete base, *Boatabode* will make and store all its electricity. The translucent skin will daylight the interior, open up to cooling winds, and get layered with seasonal insulation.

Resembling neither boat nor house, it will be a lofty tent secured to a heavy raft. The raft will be a reinforced concrete-and-Styrofoam platform about sixteen feet wide and 40 to 60 feet long. Stretched over the platform will be a *tensile membrane structure*—a shelter formed by architectural textiles held taut by a metal framework. Using a series of arching ribs, the tent will enclose a single arched volume, about sixteen feet high. An aluminum and steel exoskeleton will hold the tent firm in storms, as it serves as maintenance scaffolding and trelliswork.

Much of the character of *Boatabode* will depend on the *guided vegetation* (pruned annual and perennial vines) it grows on its exoskeleton. The vines will make shade and fruit in the summer, and look gnarly in winter. The vines will include architectural vines (wisteria, grape) and food vines (grape, tomato, pumpkin, bean).

The steel structure will support retractable gangways, decks, and a rooftop viewing deck made of aluminum grating. These metal sections will unfold towards the best views and weather, into the available slip space. At each

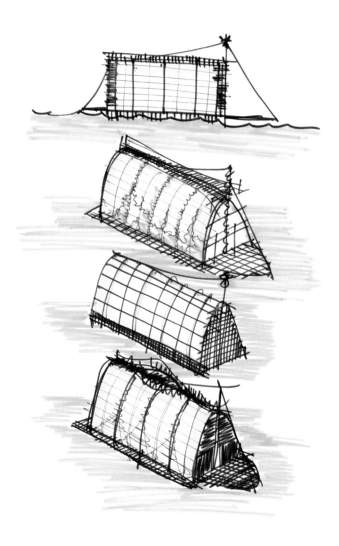

end of the tent a window wall made of glass and polycarbonate panels will be outfitted with sliding doors and operable windows. One end will contain a huge arch-shaped view of the outdoors.

The tent holds four capsules: *play, sleep, write, function.* (Think of huge, insulated Colman coolers.) Each is a rollable micro-environment with separate controls. The *play* and *function* capsules stack over the *sleep* capsule, forming a two-level tower at the dock end of the *Boatabode.* The *write* capsule is free-wheeling.

The *play* capsule has two chambers: kitchen, and shower room with sink. Cabinetry and shower are made of bright, resin-coated textiles designed to make playing with food and water more fun.

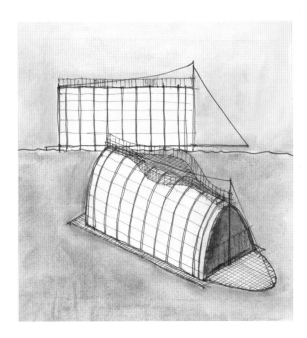

The *function* capsule has three chambers: Two chambers hold composting toilets. One space holds equipment for purifying local salt or freshwater or for reusing graywater and rain, and for pumping water and storing it. Another space holds electrical equipment.

The *sleep* capsule is inspired by the bed-sized room of Japanese capsule hotels. You adjust the ambience: light, temperature, humidity, fragrance, and acoustics. The insulated, lockable capsule makes it possible to sleep in a tent in a noisy marina. Weather permitting, two roofs—capsule top and tent skin—can be opened to the sky.

The *write* capsule will be like a VW bug—shiny, compact, and mobile—that can wheel around the tent and roll onto the deck. You can fling open all "doors" or close them for acoustical and thermal coziness to read, write, think, phone, or watch movies in a private cockpit of compact machinery. (Maybe you can drive this capsule away when you leave home for long periods.)

In addition to the four capsules are two "rolling boulders." Each is a free-form, hard plastic base holding books and soft cushions, with storage space concealed. Two long, weather-resistant tables also roll around, inside or out, for dining and work.

Why so much mobility? Why not? The idea is not only to seize the day, but to follow the sun.

floating lodging in north america

Canadian Princess Resort: Permanently moored in Ucluelet Harbour on Vancouver Island, this retired hydrographic survey ship is a floating hotel and center for ocean-fishing and whale watching. www.canadianprincess.com

Canoe Pass Inn: A floating, two-suite bed and breakfast at the mouth of the Fraser River. www.canoepassinn.com

Clayoquot Resorts: A 16-room wilderness resort—in Quait Bay on Clayoquot Sound—offering all the outdoor attractions of British Columbia, from a very luxurious base: a floating lodge. www.wildretreat.com

Harborside Hotel and Marina: Moderately-priced motel rooms floating on Garrison Bight, the bay harboring Key West's main houseboat marinas. keywestharborside.com

King Pacific Lodge: This exclusive wilderness resort—towed each summer into remote Barnard Harbour, off Princess Royal Island, B.C.—has posh dining and lounge spaces and encompasses seventeen fancy guest suites in a floating lodge. Built on a giant Navy barge and billed as the "most luxurious wilderness lodge ever built," it is made of local stone and massive timbers. Float planes fly in guests for fishing, hiking, sea kayaking, and other leisure activities. Largest guest-caught fish to date: a 171-pound Halibut. www.kingpacificlodge.com

Knight Inlet Lodge: Located on Glendale Cove—one of the densest nodes of grizzly bears in British Columbia—the Lodge looks like a floating village. Bear and Orca-viewing tours are organized. www.knightinletlodge.com

River Run Cottages: A small bed and breakfast—with one floating cottage, *The Waterlily*—set on a rustic river-front in a casual neighborhood of floating houses. www.riverruncottages.com

FLOATING HOME RENTALS
Sea Village, New Jersey
www.seavillage.com

Real estate offices: Most cities with residential marinas have real estate agents that specialize in floating home sales, leases, and rentals.

Marina offices, dock bulletin boards, Web sites, and word-of-mouth reveal renting and leasing opportunities. Houseboat owners, especially those in Sausalito, tend to travel.

bibliography

Condor, Russell. *Handmade Houseboats: Independent Living Afloat.* Camden, Maine: Ragged Mountain Press, 1992.

Dennis, Ben and Betsy Case. *Houseboat.* Seattle: Smuggler's Cove Publishing, 1977.

Dubin, Beverly. *Water Squatters.* Santa Barbara: Capra Press,1975.

Gabor, Mark. *Houseboats.* New York: Ballantine Books, 1979.

Laturnus, Ted. *Floating Homes: A Housebook Handbook.* British Columbia: Harbour Publishing, 1986.

Maté, Ferenc. *Waterhouses: The Romantic Alternative.* Vancouver, British Columbia: Albatross Publishing House, 1977.

Newcomb, Duane. *The Wonderful World of Houseboating.* Englewood Cliffs, New Jersey: Prentice-Hall, 1974.

index

Note: Page numbers in *italic* refer to photographs and illustrations.

PHOTO CREDITS

All photographs © Andrew Garn, except as noted below

© Attika Architekten: pp. 184-187
© Erwin & Peggy Bauer: p. 35 (upper right and lower left)
Courtesy Belvedere-Tiburon Landmarks Society: pp. 41-42
Courtesy City Archives, Vancouver, British Columbia: p. 40
© Tor Eigeland: p. 37
© John Elk III: p. 37
© Barbara Flanagan pp. 25 (lower left), 60, 62, 188-189
Courtesy Library of Congress, © William Henry Jackson: p. 33
© John Lamb/Getty Images: p. 39
Courtesy Library of Congress (unidentified photographer): p. 42 (top)
© Craig Lowell/Eagle Visions: p. 35 (lower right)
© Andrea Pistolesi: pp. 32, 35 (upper left)